Hamlyn all-colour paperbacks

David Saunders

Seabirds

illustrated by Ken Lilly

Hamlyn · London
Sun Books · Melbourne

FOREWORD

Seabirds are an ubiquitous group with a distribution of species from the high polar regions to the tropics. Although some have a restricted distribution, many are wide-ranging so that they occur in several continents. Thus an observer in the southern hemisphere will be quite familiar with a number of species which occur, or have close relatives, in the northern hemisphere. Some may nest only in one part of the world but move long distances during the winter season, while others may have a much wider breeding distribution. This, together with the fact that in many cases a naturalist may have to travel to remote islands or distant headlands, helps to create an aura of excitement, magic and drama which no other group of birds can match.

Within the scope of this book it is, of course, not possible to enter into any great detail concerning the world's seabirds, small as their number may be in comparison with that of landbirds. Nor is this book meant to serve as an identification manual for seabirds. It is, rather, an attempt to produce a broad account of the world's seabirds, drawing the reader's attention to their many absorbing facets. By doing so I hope that more people will be encouraged to take an interest in seabirds, and obtain the enjoyment that I and many others gain from watching them. By these means, those species which are in danger for a variety of reasons may come to enjoy a greater measure of public sympathy and understanding so that the necessary conservation measures can be taken whenever possible.

D.S.

Published by the Hamlyn Publishing Group Limited
London · New York · Sydney · Toronto
Hamlyn House, Feltham, Middlesex, England
In association with Sun Books Pty Ltd., Melbourne
Copyright © The Hamlyn Publishing Group Limited 1971
ISBN 0 600 10073 1
Phototypeset by Filmtype Services Limited, Scarborough
Colour separations by Schwitter Limited, Zurich
Printed in Holland by Smeets, Weert

CONTENTS

	Millions of years	Ratites	Tinamous	Grebes	Divers	Penguins	Tube-nosed swimmers	Pelicans and allies
PLEISTOCENE								
PLIOCENE	10							
MIOCENE	20							
	30							
OLIGOCENE	40							
	50							
EOCENE	60							
PALEOCENE	70							
	80							
UPPER CRETACEOUS	90							
	100							

WHAT IS A SEABIRD

The name seabird is a rather vague term and just what species of birds may be classed under it depends on an individual's own ideas and opinions. Most people would agree, however, that seabirds belong to four separate orders of birds.

The order Sphenisciformes contains the penguins. The Procellariiformes includes the albatrosses, petrels and related species. The Pelecaniformes includes the gannets, pelicans and several other closely related families. Finally the Charadriiformes, a large order, contains many diverse families including the skuas, gulls, terns and auks.

The landbirds are, however, much more widely represented,

The relative age of the different orders of birds

being found in twenty-eight different orders, many of which can be divided into numerous suborders. The seabirds of the world are represented by only a few orders and families and relatively few species, although many have enormous populations; indeed, some colonies may be measured in millions. Of the 8,600 or so species known at the present time only 285 may be considered as seabirds, and some of these are more birds of inland waters than the sea. While it is likely that a few more new and obscure species of landbird may be discovered, it is not considered that any new seabird species will be announced to science.

The one family of Sphenisciformes

The four orders in which the world's seabirds are placed may be divided into fifteen families.

The penguins all belong to a single family, the Spheniscidae, and are only found in the southern hemisphere, though one species reaches tropical regions at the Galapagos Islands.

The Procellariiformes may be divided into four families. The Diomedeidae contains the albatrosses which, except for three North Pacific species, are all birds of southern oceans, rarely wandering into the North Atlantic. Two families, the Hydrobatidae and the Procellariidae, contain the petrels and shearwaters of the world, of which the vast majority are found in the southern hemisphere, in particular the South Pacific. The four diving petrels of the family Pelecanoididae are all restricted to southern oceans.

The five families of Pelecaniformes

The four families of Procellariiformes

The Pelecaniformes may be divided into six families of which five are seabirds: the Phaëthontidae – tropicbirds, the Pelecanidae – pelicans, the Sulidae – gannets, the Phalacrocoracidae – cormorants, and the Fregatidae – frigatebirds. Once again they are all concentrated in the southern region.

The Charadriiformes contains seventeen families of which five are seabirds. The Stercorariidae, a small family contains the skuas. The gulls and terns are often grouped together as the Laridae, but in this case the terns are treated separately as the Sternidae. The latter are found fairly evenly throughout the world, but the gulls, however, have spread from northern regions where they are particularly well represented. The three species of skimmer – the Rynchopidae – are all tropical birds. The auks or Alcidae are all restricted to northern waters.

The five families of Charadiiformes

DISTRIBUTION OF SEABIRDS

Although certain areas of the world contain more seabirds than others, even within these areas there will be found a greater or lesser abundance of birds, both in terms of species and overall abundance. Considering that the oceans account for some seventy per cent of the surface area of the globe, the number of seabird species is surprisingly small. On the other hand, some of the most numerous birds in the world are probably seabirds. Charles Darwin writing in the *Origin of Species* considered the Fulmar Petrel (*Fulmarus glacialis*) to be the most numerous bird in the world. However, more recent studies have shown that this is not the case, and the title might well be claimed with some justification by another petrel – Wilson's Petrel (*Oceanites oceanicus*).

Some large areas of the oceans are virtually devoid of bird life and are in effect 'avian deserts'. These are generally in regions where the circulation of wind and currents is such that a zone free of any movement is created. One such area is the well-known Sargasso Sea. The absence of turbulence

Upwelling regions

Drift of warm surface water away from land in subtropics

Sea

Cooler water from depths comes to surface in such areas

Land

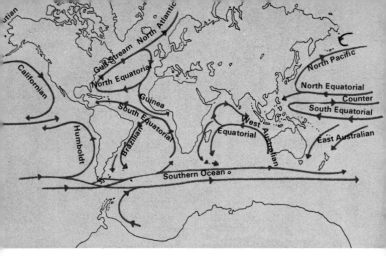

Ocean currents

means that mineral salts, if present, are not brought into the surface-water layers. Without these nutrients plankton cannot form, so without the primary link in the food chain there is a corresponding absence of fish and the birds which prey on them for their chief source of food.

The rotation of the earth causes currents to flow clockwise in the northern hemisphere and anti-clockwise in the south. The effect of these is to bring water from one region to the coasts of another, where a vertical mixing will take place as the water begins to 'pile up'. The same action will take place in the region from which the water has drifted. In this case the deeper layers will be brought to the surface. The effect of all this upwelling and turbulence is to ensure that nutrients are brought to the surface and dispersed. These may be concentrated in some areas by currents, while in others such material will be scanty or non-existent.

These upwellings occur in well-known places, for instance, off West Africa in the Canary Current and off South America in the Humboldt Current. Such upwellings of cooler water mean that some species can exist much further north into tropical waters than would otherwise be possible, and it is in such plankton-rich areas that the largest communities of seabirds will be found.

The distribution of seabirds in the world's oceans is of interest. The largest concentration is found in the Pacific, where nearly half the species may be seen. Next comes the Atlantic, followed by the Indian, Antarctic and Arctic Oceans and the Mediterranean Sea.

The distribution of seabirds in an area may be divided into three sectors – inshore, offshore and pelagic. Some species may be restricted throughout their range to one or other of these, while others may, for example, be inshore feeders during the breeding season, but otherwise roam the oceans.

Some seabirds may be very restricted in range while others are found throughout the world. One of the most widespread is the Caspian Tern (*Hydroprogne tschegrava*). As can be seen from the accompanying map, this large and handsome species of tern has a wide, though scattered, distribution throughout the world. It is to be found both on the coast and far inland, being only absent as a breeding species from South America. The inference from such a widespread and disrupted breeding range is that the Caspian Tern is an ancient species. Its breeding range may have been larger and more continuous than it is today, disturbance by man being a valid reason for the disintegration.

Other seabirds have wide ranges besides the Caspian Tern, though unlike some landbirds none seems to have been introduced into new areas. The Roseate Tern (*Sterna dougalli*) is another widespread tern, though again it is not found nesting in South America. Unlike the last species, the Roseate is very much a bird of coasts and islands for breeding. Even though it is widespread, it is not a very common species.

Some species like the Black-headed Gull (*Larus ridibundus*) may be very widespread in one region, in this case Europe and Asia, but only a rare visitor elsewhere. Others may breed in one zone, yet move vast distances during the off-season to feed in another. The Wilson's Petrel is an excellent example of this type. It breeds in the Antarctic regions and comes north into the North Pacific and Atlantic during the polar winter.

Although quite a number of seabird species are wide-ranging and almost universal in their choice of breeding and

Caspian Tern and map showing its distribution

feeding areas, others are of a very restricted nature. The Audouin's Gull (*L. audouinii*) is a typical example. As can be seen from the map, it is only found on a scattering of islands within the Mediterranean zone, while the actual number of pairs is little more than 1,000. It is a species which seems to be vanishing as breeding areas become more prone to disturbance. Another possible danger to its continued existence is predation of its eggs and chicks by other gull species.

The Mediterranean Black-headed Gull (*L. melanocephalus*) must also be considered as a vanishing species. It is restricted to the eastern Mediterranean and the Black Sea, while there is a report by the explorer Sven Hedinn of an isolated breeding population in central Asia. Unlike Audouin's Gull, this species does wander further afield and occurs almost annually in Great Britain, among other places.

The Waved Albatross (*Diomedea irrorata*), although only found nesting on one island in the Galapagos Islands off Ecuador, wanders far across the Pacific while an immature or during the off-season. Another species restricted entirely to the Galapagos Islands is the Flightless Cormorant (*Nannopterum harrisi*). Unlike the albatross, the cormorant does not wander from its breeding islands but stays within the same region throughout its life. Since it does not need to fly, this bird has lost the use of its wings and, indeed, has undergone other significant changes.

Distribution of Audouin's Gull

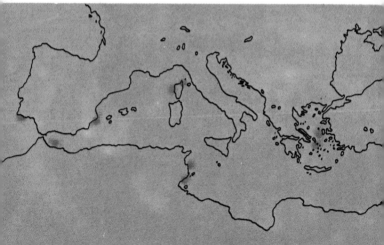

Where birds are so restricted in their breeding range the danger is that they could quickly become extinct. For example, the Great Auk (*Pinguinus impennis*), a restricted species in the sense that it was flightless, was bludgeoned into extinction to satisfy man's greed. In these, one hopes, more enlightened days this will not be allowed to happen again. However, this is no safeguard against changes in an ocean current or the occurrence of a natural disaster which might so alter the ecology of an area that a species of a restricted nature could quickly be lost to the world.

Many seabird species may be divided into subspecies, and some have several. A subspecies is one which may be distinguished from other populations of the same species. Because of differences of opinion among taxonomists the number of subspecies is constantly changing. As this leads to some confusion

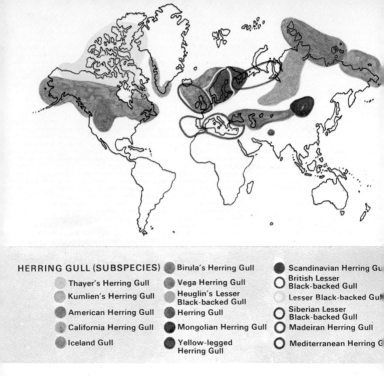

Distribution of the Herring Gull and its subspecies

among ornithologists, throughout the rest of the book there will be no reference to subspecific forms.

One particular example of the sort of chaos that can result may be seen in the cases of the Herring Gull (*Larus argentatus*) and Lesser Black-backed Gull (*L. fuscus*). In both the New World and the Old there are a number of other gulls, sometimes considered as full species, sometimes only with a subspecific rank, which come into the same grouping.

Starting with Birula's Herring Gull (*L. a. birulai*), a central Siberian bird, there are two chains of subspecies which circle the polar basin to meet in overlapping links. Where this overlap occurs 'Herring Gulls' and 'Lesser Black-backed Gulls' may be found. One such zone is western Europe where the two gulls behave as different species. They are not only different in colour but in their habits as well. However, interbreeding

14

between the two has been recorded on several occasions.

The Herring Gull tends to be a sedentary bird, normally not wandering great distances from its natal area. It often breeds on cliffs and cliff slopes as well as on level ground. The Lesser Black-backed Gull, easily distinguished by its darker mantle and yellow legs, is a migratory species. Most leave their northern quarters during the winter months for Iberia and West Africa. Their breeding colonies which are re-occupied during February and March are usually on more level ground, often far inland. In feeding habits the species differ in some respects; for instance, the Herring Gull is much more of a scavenger.

The chains of Herring Gulls vary from each other in shade of colour, both of plumage and of bill and legs. Most seem to have discrete breeding areas, though where these overlap hybrids occur. The palest of all is the Iceland Gull (*L. glaucoides*) though, as if to add more confusion, it does not nest in Iceland!

(Top to bottom) Iceland Gull, British Herring Gull, Yellow-legged Gull, Lesser Black-backed Gull

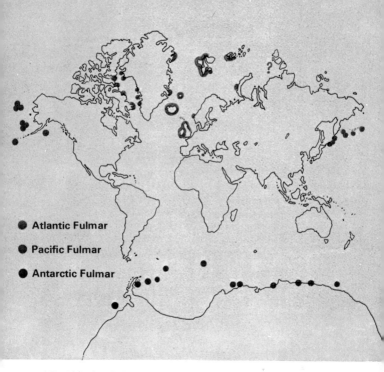

● Atlantic Fulmar

● Pacific Fulmar

● Antarctic Fulmar

Map showing Fulmar distribution

In any species there may be a marked change in size from one part of its range to another. This is called a cline, a term first used by Sir Julian Huxley in 1939. Individuals from either end of the range may differ so considerably from one another that they are given subspecific rank. The changes throughout the range may not be gradual or even, but rather occur in a series of jumps or steps.

Three 'rules' have been formulated. The first, Bergmann's rule, states that 'body size tends to be larger in the cooler parts of the total range and smaller in the warmer parts'. Thus, animals in the far north will be larger than those of the same species further south.

That known as Allen's rule states that 'extensions of the body (in birds, chiefly bills) tend to be longer in the warmer

(Top to bottom)
Antarctic Fulmar,
Pacific Fulmar,
Atlantic Fulmar

parts of the total range and shorter in the cooler parts'. The larger-bodied animals in the north have less surface area in relation to weight, so that heat loss is not so rapid. As a further adaptation, appendages which might lose heat in the north are also reduced in size.

Gloger's rule states that 'in a more humid region animals will be darker pigmented than those in the dry areas'.

There will also be clines in such things as bill shape. A good example of this is to be found in the Fulmar Petrel. Those from the Antarctic have slender bills, while in the North Pacific bills are slightly larger. Crossing now into the Arctic/Atlantic area we find bills which are stouter still, most particularly in the north-east of the region.

THE SEABIRD GROUPS

Penguins

Who, on visiting a zoo or looking at the pictures in a book, sees these birds and fails to be captivated by them? Perhaps this is because we tend to see in them various human characteristics, particularly their upright stance and inquisitive nature.

Restricted to the southern hemisphere, though by no means to the polar regions as is the popular conception, some eighteen species of penguins have been described. The largest of all is the Emperor Penguin (*Aptenodytes forsteri*) which in peak condition can weigh as much as 41 kg, though it normally averages 30 kg, and is nearly 122 cm (4 ft) in height. The other species range in size down to the Fairy, Little or Little Blue Penguin (*Eudyptula minor*) of Australia and New Zealand.

Fossil remains, again restricted to the southern hemisphere, show that larger species existed at one time. At least one of these, now named *Pachydyptes ponderous*, stood about 152 cm (5 ft) high. Why this species and others which we know from their fossil records died out is impossible to tell. Those remains so far discovered seem to indicate a bone structure and general appearance similar to that of species alive today. Information as to earlier members of the order is still not available, though perhaps as a guide we may turn to the auks of the northern hemisphere and the diving petrels of the south. Members of both groups use their wings as paddles under water; the wings are stunted so that during flight they need to be flapped vigorously, while in calm weather take-off from the sea is anything but easy.

Penguins, their powers of flight long lost, their wings flattened to strong narrow flippers, have adapted themselves even further to their environment. Their torpedo-like bodies can be projected through the water at speeds of up to ten knots, the tail and feet being used as rudders. Quite often the mode of travel is by 'porpoising', the bird breaking clear of the surface while inhaling air prior to diving beneath to swim for several more yards. On land penguins spend most of their time in an upright position, though in snow some species occasionally flop down on their bellies and 'toboggan' using their feet and flippers to propel them.

Relative sizes of Miocene penguin, Man, Emperor, Adelie and Little Penguins

6

5

4

3

2

1

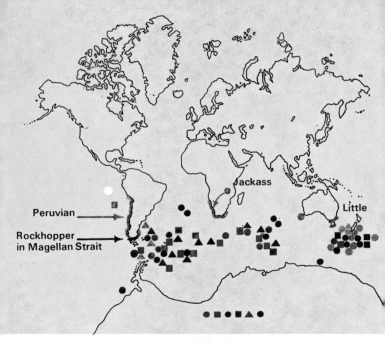

Distribution of various penguin species

The plumage of penguins, unlike that of most birds, covers the whole body; it is also very short and dense. The longest feathers are those belonging to the Emperor Penguin, yet these barely reach 8 cm (3½ in) in length, while in some of the smaller species they do not exceed 2 cm (1 in). Beneath this dense over-coat of feathers a thick layer of blubber or fat is to be found which not only provides extra insulation for the body, but is a storage organ for both food and water as well.

Penguins feed generally on animals caught close to the surface of the sea within easy reach of the shore. The larger species feed on squid which abound in Antarctic waters, though no doubt they supplement their diet with fish. Those species which range further north seem to eat large quantities of small fish and it has been estimated that four-fifths of the food taken by the Black-footed or Jackass Penguin (*Spheniscus demersus*) off south-west Africa is of this nature. Each penguin requires an average of 250 gm of food a day, so that in a year the

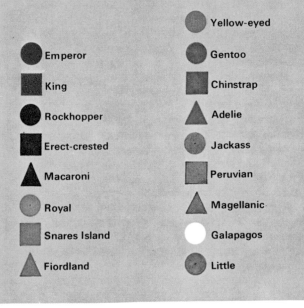

Emperor

King

Rockhopper

Erect-crested

Macaroni

Royal

Snares Island

Fiordland

Yellow-eyed

Gentoo

Chinstrap

Adelie

Jackass

Peruvian

Magellanic

Galapagos

Little

population of Black-footed Penguins, numbering some 100,000 birds, may consume 6,000 tons of fish. An increase in human fishing activity in the area could seriously affect the penguins by diminishing their food supply.

Krill, the name given to the shrimp-like crustaceans *Euphausia superba*, which in their countless billions stain red the surface of Antarctic seas in certain seasons, provides a welcome source of food. The droppings of birds which feed on these organisms are stained bright red. With man's wanton destruction of the great whales the amount of krill now available has vastly increased and may account for the colonization of new areas by the Chinstrap Penguin (*Pygoscelis antarctica*).

A possible serious menace to penguin colonies is that of disturbance by man, and this can even take place in the far frozen south unless special care is taken. With the advent of tourism in the Antarctic, disturbance at penguin colonies must be avoided at all costs.

The two species of Penguin which extend their range furthest south are the Emperor Penguin and the Adelie Penguin (*P. adeliae*), the latter named by the French explorer Dumont d' Urville in honour of his wife, Adélie.

The Emperor is restricted to the coasts of the Antarctic continent, while the Adelie, although found on the mainland, also extends northwards to islands like the South Shetlands, South Orkneys and South Sandwich Islands.

Some twenty or so colonies of Emperor Penguins are known, the largest being that on Coulman Island in the Ross Sea where 100,000 birds congregate, a fifth of the world's total. The first Emperor Penguins were caught by members of Sir James Clark Ross's expedition in 1842, but it was not until 1902 that the first breeding colony was discovered. This was found on Cape Crozier by the men of Captain Scott's 'Discovery' expedition who were amazed to see young birds in down, meaning that incubation had taken place during the polar night.

At that time penguins were considered to be very primitive birds and a study of chick embryos was thought might lead to information concerning the origin of birds. Consequently, on Scott's second polar expedition in 1910 Edward Wilson, 'Birdie' Bowers and Apsley Cherry-Garrard man-hauled their sledges under appalling conditions through the darkness and biting winds of the Antarctic winter to Cape Crozier. For all this, the embryos which were brought back on examination revealed little which was not already known.

Only the male Emperor Penguin incubates the single egg, which takes sixty-four days to hatch. During this time the females are at the open sea which may be up to 100 miles away across the ice. The chicks are fed first by the males on a crop secretion, after which the females take over while their mates go to sea. Towards the end of the fledging period both parents assist in the feeding, though the chicks leave to fend for themselves before they are fully grown. At this stage the juveniles congregate at the edge of the ice shelf, often commencing their northern journey on an ice floe, until, on assuming their final coat of feathers, they are able to enter the sea.

Emperor Penguin and chick (left), Adelie Penguin and chick

King Penguin

In the sub-Antarctic zone, a region of remote islands and howling westerly gales, several other penguin species are found. The largest of these is the King Penguin (*Aptenodytes patagonica*), a familiar figure in zoos throughout the world. It is half the weight of its close relative the Emperor Penguin, though only 30 cm (1 ft) less in height.

The nesting site of this species is usually on bare, muddy ground close to the shore. A single egg is laid, both parents sharing the incubation which is carried out with the egg balanced on the upper surface of the adult's feet. The incubation period is about fifty-four days, after which both parents feed the chick which grows rapidly throughout the southern autumn. Clad in its thick eiderdown it faces the long winter at the nest site, living on stored fat reserves and receiving the occasional feed. During this period the smaller and weaker chicks die, while even the healthy ones lose half their autumn weight. With the onset of spring, feeding recommences and

Ringed Penguin (top), and Gentoo Penguin in pursuit of fish

the chicks, now moulting their brown down, begin to leave the colony. If parents have lost an egg or chick they will re-lay during the spring, while those that have been more successful wait until the following season. Many will therefore only breed twice in three years, laying eggs early in one season and late in another.

Other sub-Antarctic species include the Gentoo Penguin (*P. papua*) which occurs in several subspecies throughout its range, and the Chinstrap Penguin. Gentoos are mild-natured, the Chinstraps belligerent and, as if to emphasize this, the more noisy.

Both species resort to huge, crowded colonies, nesting close together. Nests are built from accumulations of stone and other debris, while Gentoos occurring furthest north can afford the comparative luxury of clumps of tussock grass. Two white eggs are usually laid, both parents taking part in the incubation which lasts about thirty-five days.

As one proceeds further north so other penguin species are encountered, among them the six members of the genus Eudyptes. All have distinct crests, yellow in colour, and it is the arrangement of these that provides an identification guide to the species involved.

Four of the species have a somewhat restricted range: the Royal Penguin (*E. schlegeli*) is only found on Macquarie Island; the Erect-crested Penguin (*E. sclateri*) occurs on the Antipodes, Bounty and Campbell Islands; the Snares Island Penguin (*E. robustus*) is restricted to the archipelago south of New Zealand which bears this name, while the Fiordland Penguin (*E. pachyrhynchus*) resides on the deeply indented coast at the southern end of South Island, New Zealand. The other two species are much more wide-ranging. The Macaroni Penguin (*E. chrysolophus*) is found southwards in the subpolar regions, while the Rockhopper (*E. crestatus*) extends as far north as the Falkland Islands and Tristan da Cunha.

The members of this group spend a good deal of their time away from the nesting colonies which may be deserted for up to five months of the year. The birds congregate for nesting in vast avian metropolises – up to 2,000,000 Royal Penguins nest on Macquarie Island – while there are also large numbers of non-breeding immatures present, the birds maturing at between five and seven years of age. Two eggs are laid but only the larger, second egg is incubated. Both sexes take part in the incubation which lasts for thirty-five days.

Other warmer clime species include the Little, Little Blue or Fairy Penguin which nests as far north as Sydney, Australia. It nests in burrows and crevices, even under coastal bungalows, and may walk up to a mile inland to find a suitable site. Because of habitat destruction and predation by animals like cats and ferrets the bird has decreased in some areas. Two, sometimes three, eggs are laid, incubation being carried out by both parents. The chicks hatch between the thirty-third and fortieth day and are guarded by each parent in turn, the off-duty bird bringing back food at night. The young birds leave for the sea by the time they are eight to nine weeks old.

Jackass Penguin (top), Little Penguin (bottom left) and White-flippered Penguin

Four species of penguins, all belonging to the genus *Spheniscus*, range further north than any other species. The Magellanic Penguin (*S. magellanicus*) inhabits the bleak coasts and islands around the southern tip of South America, including the Falkland Islands. Further north the Peruvian or Humboldt Penguin (*S. homboldti*) makes use of the cool, food-rich waters of the Humboldt Current and is found to within five degrees of the Equator. Off south-west Africa, the Black-footed or Jackass Penguin thrives in large colonies making use of the cool Benegula current.

The rarest of all is the Galapagos Penguin (*S. mendiculus*), restricted, as its name suggests, to the Galapagos Islands. Here some 500 pairs reside on Albemarle and Narborough Islands, within a degree and a half of the Equator. Their very existence in the area is dependent on the cool currents swinging out from the South American shore, a continuation of those which

Magellanic (left) and Peruvian Penguins

enable the Peruvian Penguin to come so far north. The Galapagos Penguin seeks rock crevices and caverns as nesting sites, usually close to the water's edge in sheltered bays. It usually lays two eggs.

The other three species also nest in burrows and crevices, two eggs being the normal number laid. The incubation period seems to be about four weeks and in the case of the Black-footed Penguin the chicks may be fed for up to three months.

Two species of penguins are, or were, important producers of guano, the nitrogen-rich accumulated dung at the large seabird colonies. Off Peru whole islands were stripped haphazardly of this important asset so that the nest sites of some species which burrow in the beds of accumulated droppings, notably the Peruvian Penguin, were destroyed. As much as 5,500 tons of guano produced by the Black-footed Penguin is still taken annually from the South African colonies.

Galapagos Penguin under water

Wandering Albatross in flight and on land

Albatrosses

The thirteen species of albatrosses which exist at the present time are all truly pelagic birds, notable for their large size and powers of flight. They occur in two genera – *Diomedea*, containing eleven species, and *Phoebetria* with two. The order Procellariiformes to which albatrosses belong also includes the smaller shearwaters and petrels described later.

An albatross is a stoutly built bird which on the ground looks rather ugly, a fact perhaps due to the large head and bill. The latter is most characteristic and may reach up to 15 cm (6 in) in length. The tip is hooked and instead of a single sheath as in most birds the bill is covered by horny plates. The sexes are generally alike, except in the case of the Wandering

Albatross (*D. exulans*) where the female has a dark crown cap. The birds are rather ungainly when ashore owing to the fact that their short legs are placed far back on the body so that they waddle rather than walk.

Probably because of this clumsiness when on land, sailors have given them names like 'goony- or gony-birds', 'gony' being an English dialect name for 'simple person'. Other names include 'mollymawk' or 'mollyhawk', a term which sometimes includes other maritime species like skuas and immature gulls. These names seem to be derived from the Dutch *mollemuck, mol* meaning foolish and *mok* a gull.

The long wings of the albatross enable it to spend a great part of its life at sea, gliding for what seems like hours on almost motionless wings. The largest species, the Wandering Albatross, has a wingspan of 370 cm (12 ft), the largest wingspan of any bird, though it is not the largest in overall dimensions. An albatross, using its broad feet which project beyond the tail as a rudder, can glide as swiftly across the wind as with it. The troughs and crests of the waves create air currents of which the birds take advantage to gain height swiftly before swooping low to repeat the procedure. As they often live in areas where strong winds are prevalent, albatrosses are able to use this gliding ability to a remarkable degree. If the wind drops a somewhat laboured flapping flight is adopted.

Distribution of various albatrosses

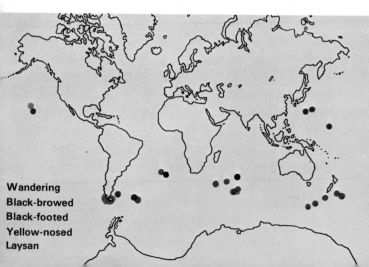

Wandering
Black-browed
Black-footed
Yellow-nosed
Laysan

Albatrosses are for the most part colonial birds when nesting, and some congregations may be very large indeed. The nest may be nothing more than a depression in the ground, though some species accumulate quite a mound of vegetable debris. In this a single egg is laid, mainly white with a few darker speckles.

Both sexes take part in the incubation which generally lasts about seventy days. The chicks are already covered in down when hatched and during the early stages are brooded continuously. The chicks are fed on regurgitated fish brought back to the nest by both parents, and on this rich diet growth is rapid. In the case of the Wandering Albatross a three-month-old chick may weigh as much as an adult. By this time the chicks are being left unguarded and feeds become somewhat erratic. There is evidence to suggest that the parent birds may wander tremendous distances while still feeding a chick. A parent from a colony in South Georgia was recognized some 2,640 miles away, while in the North Pacific albatrosses with small chicks have been recovered 2,000 miles from the colony. When left alone, the young birds defend themselves by spitting out stomach oil at any intruder approaching too close. This habit is also found in related species like the fulmars.

The length of the breeding season in the smaller albatrosses is about five months, after which the chicks finally make their own way to the sea. In the Wandering Albatross and the Royal Albatross (*D. epomophora*) the season may extend upwards of a year. The chicks of these species finally depart from the colony about eleven months after the eggs are laid, while the adults are beginning to gather to commence another season. It seems likely that in such instances the birds may breed only once every two years.

At the beginning of the breeding season albatrosses perform quite elaborate displays which are communal in some species. In some cases this display may continue during incubation, while some performances have been noted at sea, far from the nesting colony, in which yearling birds have been observed taking part.

Courtship displays of two adult male albatrosses: (top to bottom) threat posture; bill clapping or rattling; swaying gait and sky-pointing; 'dancing' with out-stretched wings

Sooty Albatross

Ten species of albatross are found in the southern hemisphere. Most breed on remote oceanic islands but sometimes extend well south into the sub-polar regions.

The Wandering Albatross breeds in three widely separated areas: in the South Atlantic on the islands of Inaccessible, Tristan da Cunha and Gough; in the South Indian Ocean on Kerguelen, Crozets, Prince Edward and Marion Islands; and on the Auckland, Antipodes, Campbell and Macquarie Islands to the south of New Zealand. The total world population has been estimated to be in the order of 100,000 birds.

Two other species, the Yellow-nosed (*D. chlororhynchos*) and Sooty Albatrosses (*P. fusca*), also nest on Tristan da Cunha. The former closely resembles the Grey-headed Albatross (*D. chrysostoma*) which nests further south on the islands round Cape Horn. The Yellow-nosed Albatross ranges further north in the South Atlantic and is one of the species most often

Buller's Albatross (left), and Shy Albatross

seen along the shipping routes in the area.

One of the rarer and less well-known species is Buller's Albatross (*D. bulleri*) which breeds on the Snares and Chatham Islands off South Island, New Zealand, moving eastwards towards Chile and Peru during the winter months.

The food taken by albatrosses is picked off the surface of the sea or from just beneath it. Squids seem to form a large part of the diet of some species, while others eat refuse discarded at sea. Indeed, the Black-footed Albatross (*D. nigripes*) of the North Pacific is known as the feathered pig.

The movements of albatrosses have been studied by ringing in certain areas. Large numbers of Wandering Albatrosses have been ringed at colonies in South Georgia. Recoveries seem to indicate a dispersal of birds across the oceans rather than a definite migration. Long distances may be traversed; one bird was noted 9,600 km (6,000 miles) from its colony.

Laysan Albatross

Three species of albatross are found in the North Pacific: the Short-tailed (*D. albatrus*), the Laysan (*D. immutabilis*) and the Black-footed.

All are now very much more restricted in their breeding ranges than previously. The Short-tailed Albatross has been on the verge of extinction for some years. Once occurring in large numbers on islands to the south of Japan, vast numbers were killed by fishermen and by those seeking their murderous fortunes in the feather industry. Between 1887 and 1903 it is considered that 5,000,000 birds were killed on Toroshima in the Izu group, while in 1922-23 almost the whole breeding population of some 3,000 birds was exterminated. Natural hazards in the form of violent volcanic activity further decimated the colony in 1939 and again in 1941. The very survival of the species seems to have been dependent on the return of non-breeders which were away at sea when the eruptions took place. The birds are now protected by the Japanese government and in 1955 ten pairs were present, eighteen in 1958, and forty-seven birds in 1962.

The Black-footed Albatross is now confined to the Leeward Chain of the Hawaiian Islands. In 1957-58 the world popula-

Short-tailed Albatross

tion of this species was considered to be about 300,000 of which 110,000 nest in any one season.

The Laysan Albatross, also, is now restricted to the Lee-ward Chain of the Hawaiian Islands except for a few on Toroshima. The total population in 1957-58 was in the order of 1,500,000 birds of which 560,000 nest in any one year. The establishment of defence bases on certain Pacific Islands led to a conflict between service requirements and those of the birds. In spite of precautionary measures, the bird-strike problem still remains, however, and in one ten-month period damage to planes cost $83,000.

Black-footed Albatross

Like the penguin family, albatrosses have one representative restricted to the Galapagos Islands: the Waved Albatross (*D. irrorata*) which nests on Hood Island where there is a fairly stable breeding population of about 3,000 pairs. During the off-season birds range the Pacific Ocean east to the coasts of Ecuador and Peru and westwards to Japanese waters.

The albatrosses of Hood Island nest in scattered groups on the bare ground among thorn bushes and boulders, often at a distance of several hundred yards inland from the cliffs. Landing in a terrain with such obstacles is a hazardous busi-

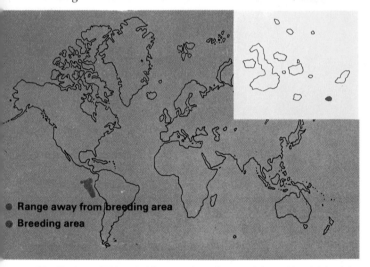

● Range away from breeding area
● Breeding area

Distribution of Waved Albatross; breeding station on Hood Island in the Galapagos (inset)

ness and Dr J. B. Nelson during his stay on the island found two birds which had died through injuries received while landing. Leg and foot wounds were quite commonplace. Taking off also presents difficulties and many birds are content to plod slowly to the cliff edge before attempting to become airborne.

The single chick on hatching is brooded by the parents for the first two weeks or so, after which it is left unguarded and seeks shelter beneath nearby bushes. Chicks seem to recognize their returning parents from the distinct call-notes given.

Waved Albatross and chick

The Waved Albatross feeds its chick on a regurgitated, rich, oily liquid made from food consumed while at sea. This method enables the birds to roam at will as, unlike many other seabirds, there is no rush to return before the food deteriorates. The chick places its beak, usually sideways, into that of the adult in order to be fed. Quite often prodigious amounts may be given at a single sitting, in fact as much as four pounds of oil, so that the chick's daily weight fluctuates greatly. Feeds become less frequent as it reaches the flying stage – usually when it is about seven months old.

One of the most interesting bird fossils ever found in England is that of an extinct albatross discovered in Suffolk during the last century. Since then similar remains have been discovered in eastern North America. It seems highly likely that before the climatic and structural changes which took place during the period of the great Ice Ages albatrosses roamed what was then the North Atlantic. Wiped out long ago, they seem to have been unable to recolonize what would appear to be an eminently satisfactory region.

The restriction on their free movement from the South Atlantic northwards seems to be the Doldrums – the area of calms – which makes an almost insurmountable barrier for species like the albatrosses. To the west, natural land barriers prevent colonization by the Pacific species.

Occasionally albatrosses are reported from the North Atlantic, and in the past such records were regarded with some scepticism as it was known that sailors kept the birds as pets during long ocean voyages. It is now many years since sailors indulged in such pursuits but albatrosses are still reported, with records increasing in recent years.

Most records seem to refer to a migratory species, the Black-browed Albatross (D. melanophris). During the southern winter it moves northwards following the cold currents towards more tropical waters and manages to cross the Equator from time to time. If enough managed to reach the North Atlantic there is no reason why, with the climate suitable and food no doubt available, the birds should not establish themselves quite easily.

There have been several indications that this could take place. Between 1860 and 1894 an albatross was regularly noted in the gannet colony on Mykines Holm in the Faroes, until it was killed by bird hunters. More recently one was seen in a gannet colony on the Westmann Islands, Iceland, while since 1967 one has been seen, to the amazement of many bird-watchers, among the gannets on the Bass Rock, Scotland.

Black-browed Albatross in flight (left) and, in foreground of picture (below), with gannets

Wilson's Petrel

Storm petrels

The twenty-two species of storm petrel are the smallest of web-footed seabirds, being similar in size to landbirds like the House Martin (*Delichon urbica*). In fact, in general appearance they rather resemble this species. Most are whitish beneath and dark above and have pale rumps. The smallest is the Least Storm Petrel (*Halocyptena microsoma*), some 13 cm (5 in) in length, which nests on islands off Lower California. Other species range in size up to 25 cm (10 in) in length.

Named, perhaps, after St Peter because the birds seem to walk on the surface of the sea during feeding, petrels often follow in the wake of ships where they pick up items of food thrown to the surface by the churning propellers. Not all species, however, have this habit. A favourite name among seamen for these birds is Mother Carey's chickens; this comes from the words Mater Cara which is an appellation of the Blessed Virgin Mary.

Who can say with any degree of certainty which is the most numerous bird in the world? A number of seabird species could perhaps lay claim to this title, among them being Wilson's Petrel (*Oceanites oceanicus*) which breeds in vast uncountable colonies at many sites in Antarctica and on sub-Antarctic islands like Kerguelen and the Falklands.

At the breeding colonies nests are to be found in cliff crevices, among boulders, on scree slopes and in burrows in the peaty soil. These sites are typical, also, for the rest of the family. The colonies are usually visited during the hours of darkness, the day being spent at sea or in the nest chamber. A single white egg is laid and both parents take part in the incubation and feeding of the chick, which is some seven weeks old when it leaves the nest. From those species studied in any detail, it is evident that the storm petrels are several years old before they return to the colonies to breed.

During the southern winter the Wilson's Petrel moves northwards into the main ocean basins, though less into the Pacific than elsewhere. There are few British sightings, though the bird is probably more numerous in this area than the records indicate, for it is frequently seen in the Bay of Biscay. On the western side of the Atlantic Wilson's Petrel is very common, often coming close inshore, though it is rarely blown inland.

Characteristic flight of Wilson's Petrel (top right) and 'pattering' on water (right)

The storm petrels are scattered throughout the world's oceans. Some, like the Wilson's Petrel already described, have a wide distribution, particularly during the winter months; others are much more restricted. Like the Grey-backed Storm Petrel (*Garrodia neresis*), some nest in the Antarctic regions and roam throughout the southern oceans, while on the other side of the world the Fork-tailed Petrel (*Oceanodroma furcata*) is to be found in the North Pacific, with colonies on the island chain of the Kuriles and Aleutians and on the west coast of North America.

Hornby's Storm Petrel (*O. hornbyi*) breeds high in the Chilean Andes, while Elliot's Storm Petrel (*O. gracilis*) is one of several species restricted to various island archipelagos in the central Pacific Ocean.

In European waters two species are found. The British Storm Petrel (*Hydrobates pelagicus*) breeds on remote islands and coasts from the Westmann Islands, Iceland, south to the Canary Islands, one of its major strongholds being islands off western Britain. Some of these undoubtedly contain colonies

Storm Petrel (top), and Elliot's Storm Petrel

with many thousands of birds but, because of the species' nocturnal nature and the difficult terrain in which it often nests, true assessments of the population are hard to come by.

Leach's Petrel (*O. leucorhoa*) is a very numerous bird on the eastern coast of North America, breeding in large colonies, perhaps in millions, on islands off the coasts of southern Labrador, Newfoundland, New Brunswick, Nova Scotia and Maine. It is also found, though only in comparatively small numbers, i.e. several thousand pairs, on several islands off north-west Britain, in the Faroes – where nesting was first proved in 1934 – and on the Westmann Islands. In the North Pacific, the bird's breeding range extends northwards from Lower California to Alaska and westwards to the Kuriles.

Another widespread species is the White-faced Storm Petrel (*Pelagodroma marina*) which nests on Tristan da Cunha, the Cape Verde Islands and the Salvages in the Atlantic Ocean, on New Amsterdam and St Pauls in the southern Indian Ocean, on the Galapagos Islands in the Pacific and at many sites round New Zealand and along the south coasts of Australia.

Striped Petrel (top) and Hornby's Storm Petrel

Fulmars

There are six species which are normally classed as fulmars, though four of these are in monotypic genera. The largest is the Giant Petrel (*Macronectes giganteus*); with a wingspan of 2 m (6½ ft) it is more the size of a small albatross. Found on a range of islands right round the Antarctic continent, the Giant Petrel occurs in two forms: the white in high latitudes, the dark in more temperate regions. A formidable bird indeed, it feeds on carcasses washed ashore, but also kills other seabirds like penguins, gulls and prions.

The Cape Pigeon (*Daption capensis*) also breeds on a range of sites round Antarctica including the Grahamland Peninsula. Although well-known to sailors in southern waters, it was not until 1903 that the first nest was found by members of the Scottish National Antarctic Expedition in South Orkney.

Two other species, the Antarctic Petrel (*Thalassoica antarctica*) and the Snow Petrel (*Pagodroma nivea*), are both restricted to the far south. The latter is almost confined to the great ice barriers and is found further south than any seabird except for the Emperor Penguin and Great Skua (*Catharacts skua*).

The Silver-grey or Antarctic Fulmar (*Fulmarus glacialoides*), breeding on the Antarctic mainland and offshore islands, is considered to be the stock from which birds crossed into the North Pacific, probably during the Ice Ages. Eventually birds passed into the North Atlantic so that the Northern Fulmar (*F. glacialis*) now occurs with a subspecies in both northern ocean basins.

In both the Pacific and Atlantic there is a variation in colour shades from light forms through intermediate to darker or 'blue' forms. In north-east Canada, Greenland, and northern islands like Novaya Zemlya and Spitzbergen the population is mainly blue. On Bear Island approximately sixty per cent are blue, while further south the bulk of the population is of the pale type. A general rule seems to be that where the sea-water temperature is above freezing in July the birds are of the light form, with the blue occurring where the sea is at or below freezing point. In the Pacific this rule is reversed.

The North Atlantic Fulmar has attracted a good deal of attention from ornithologists during the present century. In the seventeenth century Fulmars were known to be nesting

Giant Petrel (top), Cape
Pigeon (bottom left) and Silver-
grey Fulmar

south of Jan Mayen only, on Grimsay off Iceland and on the islands of St Kilda to the west of the Outer Hebrides. In the years that followed the birds began to spread round Iceland, and early in the nineteenth century the first were noted breeding on the Faroe Islands.

In 1878 birds nested on Foula, outermost of the Shetland Islands. Since that date there has been a considerable expansion right round these islands, with birds now breeding inland on ruined crofts and on stone walls in some areas. The great cliffs of Hoy in the Orkneys were colonized in 1900 and other islands in the archipelago shortly afterwards. Continuing southwards, the birds extended down the east coast of Great Britain to Norfolk where nesting was first noted in 1946. Further south still, birds continually prospect the Kent coast and will no doubt breed there soon.

In western Britain the story is similar, with birds beginning to nest in Cornwall and Devon in the 1940s following successful colonization further north. Eastwards along the south coast Fulmars are regularly seen on the Dorset, Isle of Wight and Sussex cliffs, though successful breeding has yet to be confirmed. In Ireland, following an initial colonization in North Mayo in 1911, Fulmars have now spread to most suitable cliff areas on all coasts.

Why has this occurred? Although different theories have been put forward the most probable and generally accepted has been propounded by James Fisher who has spent a lifetime studying the expansion of this remarkable bird. His hypothesis is that the birds first took advantage of the waste material available during the years of the Greenland whale fishery. As this drew to a close, so distant-water fishing commenced and once again large quantities of offal were available. The Fulmar is still spreading, though its rate of increase has slowed down.

Fulmar on land and in flight (opposite)

Map showing the rapid increase
of the Fulmar round the coast of
the British Isles

Fairy Prion (front) and Broad-billed Prion

Prions

Prions, or 'whale-birds' as they are often called because of their frequent feeding associations with these animals, are among the smaller members of the family Procellariidae and belong to the genus *Pachyptila*. This contains some six species and a number of closely related subspecies, all being so similar in size and appearance that when observed at sea they are virtually impossible to identify. Their general coloration is blue-grey on the back with white underparts and on the undersurfaces of the wings. The largest species is some 30 cm (12 in) in length.

All six prions are restricted to the southern hemisphere. The Broad-billed Prion (*Pachyptila vittata*) breeds on Tristan da Cunha, Gough Island and in New Zealand waters. Salvin's or the Medium-billed Prion (*P. salvini*) breeds on Crozet and Marion Island, while the Fairy Prion (*P. turtur*), which on occasions strays north to tropical waters, nests in the Bass Strait and off New Zealand. The Thin-billed Prion (*P. belcheri*) breeds on Kerguelen and on the Falkland Islands, while the Thick-billed or Fulmar Prion (*P. crassirostris*) nests on sub-Antarctic islands south of New Zealand, Heard and Kerguelen Islands. The last species, the Dove or Antarctic Prion (*P. desolata*), nests on the Antarctic continent at Cape Denison and islands to the north like Kerguelen, Macquarie and Heard.

Detail of prion's bill showing comb-like structures or lamellae for straining water

At breeding colonies nests may be found in burrows excavated in the peaty soil or in rock crevices. A single white egg is laid and in one of the species studied – the Dove Prion – this takes some forty-five days to hatch. Chicks are fed by both parents, nightly at first but becoming more erratic towards the end of fledging which lasts some seven weeks.

Prions feed on zooplankton in the surface layer of the sea. Their bills are adapted for a water-straining procedure by lamellae, comb-like structures on either side of the bill, particularly pronounced in the Broad-billed and Salvin's Prions.

Distribution of six species of prion

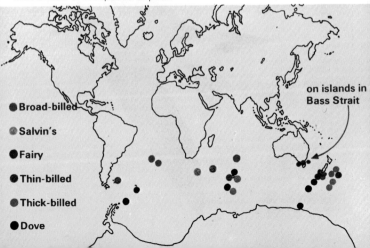

on islands in Bass Strait

- Broad-billed
- Salvin's
- Fairy
- Thin-billed
- Thick-billed
- Dove

Gadfly petrels

Gadfly petrels belong to two genera: *Bulweria* containing two species and *Pterodroma* containing twenty-five. The birds vary in size between 24 and 26 cm (9 and 10 in) in length to the largest, Schlegel's Petrel (*Pterodroma incerta*) of the South Atlantic, which is some 45 cm (18 in) long.

Some gadfly petrels, like the Great-winged Petrel (*P. macroptera*), are widely distributed. This bird breeds on many oceanic islands from Tristan da Cunha eastwards to New Zealand, and is very numerous in the southern oceans. The Kermadec Petrel (*P. phillipii*) breeds on a scattering of islands from Lord Howe in the Tasman Sea eastwards to Juan Fernandez off Chile. It is unusual in that it nests above ground under bushes and shrubs, unlike other species which resort to crevices and burrows. Others, like the Reunion Petrel (*P. aterrina*), may be restricted for breeding to a single island or archipelago.

Two of the rarest of gadfly petrels are the Bermuda Petrel or Cahow (*P. cahow*) and the Black-capped Petrel or Diablotin (*P. hasitata*), both restricted to the Caribbean region. In 1967 only twenty-two pairs of the Cahow were known to have nested, these on an island off Bermuda, and the future of this species is indeed grim. Besides being preyed upon by Yellow-billed Tropicbirds (*Phaeton lepturus*) and rats, against which

Bermuda Petrel or
Cahow in flight

Great-winged Petrel (left) and Solander's Petrel

some protection can be given, the Cahows are also threatened by the insidious menace of contamination by D.D.T. This is probably picked up by the birds when they feed on zooplankton which has absorbed the material from contaminated sea water. The birds' breeding success has also diminished alarmingly. If the situation does not improve the Cahow may well become extinct.

Distribution of the Great-winged Petrel, Solander's Petrel and Bermuda Petrel

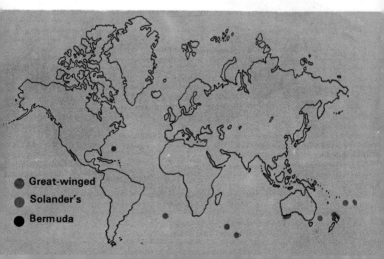

Great-winged
Solander's
Bermuda

Shearwaters

There are some twenty-one species of shearwater belonging to a number of different genera: *Puffinus* with seventeen species, *Procellaria* with three and *Adamastor* with a single member. All are long-winged and generally have slender bodies. They are so well adapted for a life at sea that they are usually awkward when ashore. In general the colour is dark above with white beneath, though some species are completely dark and one is pure white.

Most shearwaters nest in burrows or in crevices, beneath boulders, in ruined walls and even beneath buildings. Colonies may be enormous, for instance that of the Great Shearwater (*Puffinus gravis*) on the 400-acre Nightingale Island in the Tristan da Cunha group may number 3,000,000 birds. A further 300,000 nest on nearby Inaccessible, while on Gough Island a similar number may be found. These are the only

(Top to bottom)
Audubon's
Shearwater, Black-
vented Shearwater,
Sooty Shearwater,
Persian Shearwater

Audubon's Shear-
water (left) and Sooty
Shearwater in flight

breeding locations for this species which, during the southern winter, moves into the North Atlantic with quite large numbers being seen at times off the western seaboard of Europe.

Another, though more widespread, species nesting in large numbers in the southern hemisphere is the Sooty Shearwater (*P. griseus*). Its main strongholds seem to be the islands and coasts of New Zealand, with other colonies in south-east Australian waters and off the southern tip of South America. Large numbers move northwards in the off-season and in the North Atlantic the distribution is well known. The birds seem to congregate on the rich feeding grounds off the eastern United States and Canada before moving across to North European waters in July and August, finally returning southwards during the autumn months.

Most shearwaters visit their colonies at night, but not so the Audubon's Shearwater (*P. lherminieri*). At its colonies in the Galapagos Islands this bird is entirely diurnal. Studied by Dr M. P. Harris on the island of Santa Plaza off Indefatigable, the nests are mainly in boulders at the cliff base. The birds were found to nest in all months, but it appears that eggs are laid chiefly when good supplies of food – in this case zooplankton – are available, and when food is short egg-laying wanes, if it does not altogether cease.

Manx Shearwaters in flight

Of all the seabirds that breed in European waters the Manx Shearwater (*P. puffinus*) is probably the one which has received most attention from ornithologists. A bird weighing little more than 450 gm, dark grey above, white beneath, it is found only on certain islands off the western seaboard of Europe from Iceland southwards to the Azores and Madeira, with others in Bermuda. A subspecies is found in the Mediterranean and another in the Pacific Ocean.

One of the largest colonies seems to be that on Skokholm off Pembrokeshire, South Wales, where in 1968 a census showed that 35,000 pairs were nesting. On nearby Skomer another large colony is known, though no census has yet been made. The two islands together probably hold the largest concentration of Manx Shearwaters in western Europe.

It was to Skokholm that R. M. Lockley went in 1927 and in

Manx Shearwater

Nest location (left) and chick of Manx Shearwater

the years that followed much interesting work was done on the shearwater colony close to his farmhouse. This work was sadly interrupted by the war but is admirably portrayed in his book, *Shearwaters*. Since 1946 further studies have been carried out, more particularly in recent years under the direction of the Edward Grey Institute, Oxford. Large numbers of the birds have been ringed, either as chicks at the nest or by catching adults by hand at night with the aid of a torch.

From the ringing recoveries it seems that many young birds go south to Brazilian waters within a few weeks of leaving the nesting burrow. One bird wandered, or was windblown, across the southern oceans to be recovered in Australia. From all the evidence available so far it would seem that Manx Shearwaters are very long-lived birds and probably do not breed until they are five years old.

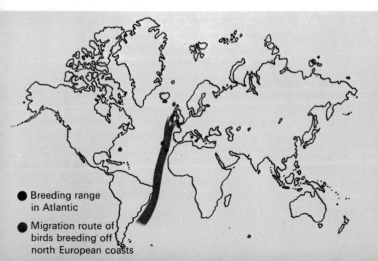

● Breeding range in Atlantic

● Migration route of birds breeding off north European coasts

Short-tailed
Shearwater or Mutton-
bird

The single, white egg is laid in late April or early May and takes fifty-two days to hatch. The chicks remain in the burrow for some ten weeks before leaving for the sea, by this time deserted by their parents. It is during this period that many chicks may be lost through both disease and predation, for they fall easy prey to marauding Great Black-backed Gulls (*Larus marinus*), as the numerous carcasses about the colonies bear silent witness.

The Short-tailed Shearwater (*P. tenuirostris*) breeds on islands off Victoria, South Australia, Tasmania and in the Bass Strait where it occurs in large colonies. Some, even on small islands, are thought to contain as many as 250,000 pairs, while the total population must measure millions of birds, making this species one of the most numerous seabirds in the world.

Rather similar to the Sooty Shearwater, which breeds in smaller numbers in the same area and much larger colonies elsewhere (see pages 54 to 55), the Short-tailed can be separated from it in the field by its smaller size and paler underwing.

Birds begin to return to their colonies during October but it is not until the latter half of November that the eggs are laid. A single, large, white egg is laid which, if lost, is not replaced during the season, a procedure found throughout the shearwater family. Incubation, which is shared by both parents, takes between fifty-three and fifty-seven days. The chick, covered with down at first, grows rapidly on the rich, though erratic, meals it receives. When it is about twelve weeks old the parents cease feeding it. The chicks remain in their burrows, fasting for up to a fortnight before they leave for the sea and begin to fend for themselves.

On leaving the breeding colonies the birds, making use of prevailing winds, head north-west across the Pacific towards Japanese waters, then, still using favourable winds, cross towards Alaska and thence south towards the United States. Now they swing away from land again on a south-westerly course which eventually returns them to the breeding area. This vast 32,000-kilometre (20,000-mile) journey is made during the off-season, and tremendous distances are covered in quite short periods; for example, one bird reached Japan, 8,800 km (5,500 miles) from its Tasmanian colony, within a month.

A local name in Australia and New Zealand is the 'mutton-bird' and the Short-tailed Shearwater figures high in the economy of some islands. Large numbers of well-grown young are taken under licence each season. After the stomach oil has been removed – for use in drugs and cosmetics – and the down plucked for sleeping bags, the birds are packed in brine barrels or canned and sold as 'Tasmanian Squab'. When cooked they have a pleasant taste, though not like that of mutton!

Migration routes of the Short-tailed Shearwater

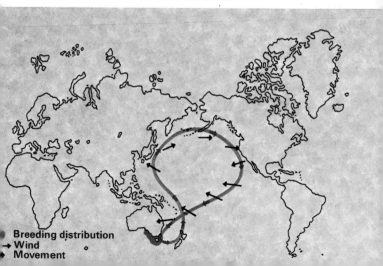

Breeding distribution
→ **Wind**
Movement

Diving petrels

The diving petrels of the family Pelecanoididae contain four species in one genus, *Pelecanoides*, and belong to the large order of Procellariiformes containing the shearwaters and petrels. They are, however, very different in appearance from these other members of the order, for with their stubby bodies, short necks and wings they closely resemble the Little Auk or Dovekie (*Plautus alle*) of Arctic seas, a similarity first noted by Charles Darwin during the voyage of the *Beagle*. This similarity is due to convergent evolution, not to a close relationship.

All four species are small and the largest, the Peruvian Diving Petrel (*P. garnotii*), does not exceed 25 cm (10 in) in length though it has double the bulk of the others. Three are very similar in appearance with glossy black plumage above and white beneath and are very difficult, if not impossible, to identify at sea. The Magellan Diving Petrel (*P. magellani*) is distinctive with white-tipped feathers on its back and wings, while two white neck patches almost form a collar. In all four the bill is black, while the legs and feet are of various shades, sometimes very bright blue.

Diving petrels are restricted to the southern hemisphere between latitudes thirty-five degrees and sixty degrees except for the Peruvian species, which extends northwards in the cool conditions of the Humboldt Current to Peru. Although they may be met at sea, often at a considerable distance from

Breeding ranges of the four species of diving petrels

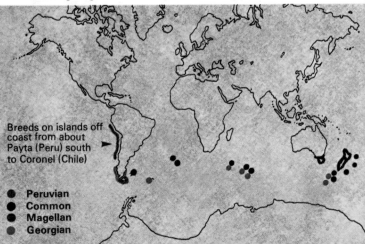

Breeds on islands off coast from about Payta (Peru) south to Coronel (Chile) ➤

- Peruvian
- Common
- Magellan
- Georgian

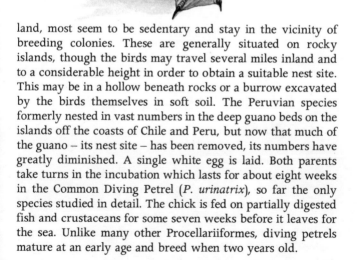

Peruvian Diving Petrel (top)
and Common Diving Petrel

land, most seem to be sedentary and stay in the vicinity of breeding colonies. These are generally situated on rocky islands, though the birds may travel several miles inland and to a considerable height in order to obtain a suitable nest site. This may be in a hollow beneath rocks or a burrow excavated by the birds themselves in soft soil. The Peruvian species formerly nested in vast numbers in the deep guano beds on the islands off the coasts of Chile and Peru, but now that much of the guano – its nest site – has been removed, its numbers have greatly diminished. A single white egg is laid. Both parents take turns in the incubation which lasts for about eight weeks in the Common Diving Petrel (*P. urinatrix*), so far the only species studied in detail. The chick is fed on partially digested fish and crustaceans for some seven weeks before it leaves for the sea. Unlike many other Procellariiformes, diving petrels mature at an early age and breed when two years old.

Georgian Diving
Petrel in flight

As we have seen, the diving petrels resemble in superficial respects the Little Auk. This latter species belongs to the Alcidae or auks, a family widely separated from the Procellariiformes and one which has no representatives in the southern hemisphere. The ecological niche used in the north by the Alcidae is filled in their absence by the diving petrels of the south. Although looking quite unlike other members of the Procellariiformes, the diving petrels do retain a number of typical characteristics such as nasal tubes and bill plates, the nostrils opening upwards side by side at the base of the bill. At the same time their size, shape, basic coloration, body weight, mode of flight and skeletal features resemble those of the Little Auk.

Diving petrels inhabit coastal waters rather than roaming the oceans like other shearwaters and petrels. Because of this, long wings and slender bodies, so necessary for sustained gliding day after day at sea, are not required and have given way to short wings and a rapid whirring flight. Like auks, groups of diving petrels may be observed flying in straight lines low across the sea or having difficulty in taking off from the surface during calm weather. Living a coastal existence enables them to visit their nest site much more frequently, and there is no need for the long periods of fasting during incubation which are undergone by many shearwaters and petrels. For the same reason, the chick may be brooded longer and fed more regularly.

Instead of finding their food on the surface of the sea or just beneath it, the diving petrels, as their name suggests, actively search for their food, crustaceans and small fish like anchovies, beneath the waves. Like the Little Auk, they will dive straight into the sea direct from flight, briefly holding their wings motionless prior to entering the water. Once beneath the surface both wings and feet are used for propulsion. The birds only remain submerged for a short period before breaking the surface and resuming their flight without a pause, often flying only a short distance before diving to feed again.

Some, if not all, of the diving petrels become flightless for a time during moult, though this does not seem to impair their agility in catching underwater prey. It is considered that the ability to use their wings beneath the surface, while at the same time being temporarily unable to fly, is an evolutionary stage which penguins must have passed through before becoming completely flightless.

Magellan Diving Petrel chasing a fish

Tropic or bo's'nbirds

The three species of tropicbirds – they are sometimes called bo's'nbirds because of their high shrilling notes which resemble those given on the boatswain's pipe – are found in tropical or subtropical seas.

The largest is the Red-tailed Tropicbird (*Phaëthon rubricauda*), found in the tropical Indian and Pacific Oceans where it occurs in a number of subspecies. Its length, not including the central tail feathers, may reach 45 cm (18 in), while the smaller Red-billed Tropicbird (*P. aethereus*) reaches 35 cm (14 in). This species occurs in the Galapagos Islands, along the west coast of Central America, the Caribbean, tropical Atlantic, Red Sea and Persian Gulf coasts. Smallest of all, 30 cm (12 in)

White-tailed Tropicbird

or so in length, is the White-tailed Tropicbird (*P. lepturus*), sometimes known as the Yellow-billed. It is found from the Caribbean eastwards through the Atlantic and Indian Oceans to the south-west Pacific.

Although tropicbirds are similar to gulls and terns in some respects their flight is rapid with quick wingbeats like that of a pigeon and quite unlike any other seabird. Food in the form of fish and squid is caught by diving just below the surface from heights of up to 15 m (50 ft).

All three species are ungainly on land because their short legs are set far back, and they therefore choose nest sites with

Red-tailed Tropicbird

easy access to the sea. A single brownish egg is laid in a bare scrape beneath rocks or vegetation. Depending on the species, this takes between forty-one and forty-five days to hatch. The chicks, which at first are covered with greyish down, grow slowly and remain in the nest for up to fifteen weeks before fledging.

Recent studies at breeding grounds have shown that a complete cycle takes from nine to twelve months on Ascension Island and ten months on the Galapagos. Because the breeding season is a disturbed affair with many egg and chick losses it may be spread throughout the year, though with distinct peaks of egg-laying at certain times.

Red-billed Tropicbird and Red-tailed Tropicbird in flight

Frigate- or 'man-o'-war birds'

Frigatebirds are probably the most aerial of all seabirds and, indeed, vie with landbirds like the swifts for being the most aerial of all birds. With their long wings they soar for hours almost without effort, seldom settling on the water. They are not adapted for life on the surface as their feet are small and have reduced webs, while their oil glands are not sufficient to prevent their plumage quickly becoming saturated.

Five species of frigatebird occur, while the precise number of subspecies – fourteen are usually listed – is still a question for debate. They are found throughout the tropical and subtropical oceans of the world, though they remain close to the vicinity of their breeding colonies. Although on occasions one may be sighted at some distance out to sea, usually the presence of frigatebirds is a sure indicator that land is close at hand.

The largest of all, the Magnificent Frigatebird (*Fregata magnificens*), has a wingspread of up to 250 cm (8 ft) and in proportion to body weight it has the biggest wingspread of any bird. Although their range is restricted to subtropical American waters with an offshoot at Cape Verde, in July, 1953, one was caught in a landing net on a small freshwater loch on Tiree, Inner Hebrides, Scotland. This is the first record of this species in the British Isles though there are a number of other North Atlantic sightings.

Distribution of the five species of frigatebirds

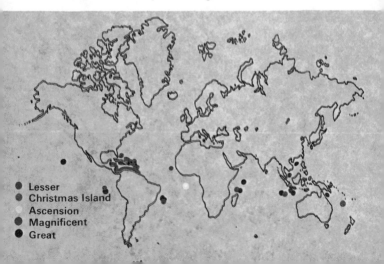

● Lesser
● Christmas Island
○ Ascension
● Magnificent
● Great

Male Magnificent Frigatebird with gular pouch inflated

The Great (*F. minor*) and Lesser Frigatebirds (*F. ariel*) are both widespread species, while the Ascension Frigatebird (*F. aquila*) is found only on Boatswain Island in the Ascension group. The last species, the Christmas Island Frigatebird (*F. andrewsi*), is restricted to Christmas Island and several other remote sites in the eastern Indian Ocean.

At some archipelagos in the central Pacific Ocean the islanders have taken advantage of the birds' apparent tameness and trained them to carry messages from island to island. Birds are trained by feeding to use perches close to buildings, and messages are carried in reed tubes attached to the wing.

Living in the tropical zone enables the birds to breed all the year round, though variations in food supply, which are probably related to weather changes, seem to ensure a definite nesting cycle.

During the courtship sessions the male develops a large, crimson gular sac or throat pouch which is inflated during display. When fully extended it obscures the whole front of the bird save for the top of the head and the eyes which just peer over. The males take up a suitable site and sit, often for hours on end, with pouch inflated, while the larger females fly overhead. As a prospective mate passes nearby the wings are spread and there is much bill rattling and harsh cackling.

Breeding colonies of frigatebirds are usually on small undisturbed islands, the nests being large untidy structures of sticks placed in anything from a low bush to a mangrove tree 20 m (60 ft) high. In the absence of suitable vegetation birds may nest on the ground. The single, large,

(Top to bottom) Lesser Frigatebird, Great Frigatebird, female Ascension Frigatebird, Christmas Island Frigatebird

white egg is incubated by both parents and hatches at between forty and fifty days. At first the chick is naked, and is
closely brooded until about two weeks old, when a growth of
down begins to afford protection. Chicks are fed on fish and
scraps regurgitated by the parents; the exact period of the
young birds' dependence is not known. They are fully fledged
after four or five months. For some considerable time after this
(it may be for as long as six months) the chicks are fed by the
parents, at the same time gradually learning through scavenging about the colony how to fend for themselves.

Colonies are often situated close to those of other seabirds,
and these provide a source of food. The frigatebird acts in an
aggressive and piratical manner (from which it no doubt de-
rives its names), chasing other species and forcing them to
drop or disgorge their food. This is then caught adeptly and
swallowed in mid-air. Another method of feeding is by swooping low over a tern colony and snatching up unguarded eggs
or chicks. Frigatebirds are able to hunt for themselves and
easily take flying fish in the air as they emerge from the waves.
Refuse floating on the surface of the sea is eagerly sought,
while newly hatched turtles making their way down a beach
provide an easy meal.

Cormorants and shags

This is a family of large seabirds with representatives in most parts of the world, including many of the great river systems of Africa and Asia. The family Phalacrocoracidae has three genera: *Phalacrocorax* with twenty-four species, *Haliëtor* with four and *Nannopterum* with a single species.

In the British Isles two species occur. The Cormorant (*P. carbo*) is a very widely distributed species and is known elsewhere in the world as the Common Cormorant. The other is the Shag (*P. aristotelis*). This name is also used as an alternative for several southern hemisphere species.

Cormorants range in size from the Pigmy Cormorant (*H. pygmeus*), some 48 cm (19 in) in length, to the Common Cormorant of about 102 cm (40 in). Cormorants are generally black or dark coloured, though some species have white underparts. They are sociable birds and gather in large colonies to nest, while non-breeding or off-duty birds often collect on favourite rocks or cliffs. Nests are usually bulky structures and several eggs are laid.

The birds are all expert divers, diving from the surface of the water by means of a distinct forward leap. Wings are generally not used under the surface, the large webbed feet being efficient propulsion units which drive the birds when necessary to a considerable depth. There are reports of fishermen having caught marine species in their nets at depths of 70

Distribution of Common Cormorant

and even 100 ft. It is thought that hearing plays an important part in the underwater search for food, a search that often brings them into conflict with human fishermen.

The Guanay Cormorant (*P. bougainvillei*) has been described as the most valuable wild bird in the world. It nests in huge colonies on islands off the coast of Chile and Peru.

The vast numbers of birds, their ranks swelled by other species like the Peruvian Booby (*Sula variegata*), feed in the plankton-rich waters of the Humboldt current and use predator-free islands for nesting. Vast quantities of droppings or guano have accumulated over thousands of years, for little rain falls to wash the material away. A Guanay Cormorant with a voracious appetite for anchovies deposits as much as 1,000 gr dry weight, of guano a month.

It was not until about 1840 that these deposits began to be seriously exploited, though previously they had been used by the Incas and other native peoples. Once governments became interested the deposits were ruthlessly stripped with no thought as to their replenishment, and species like the Peruvian Diving Petrel and Peruvian Penguin, both important guano producers, began to vanish as their nest sites were destroyed. Between 1848 and 1875 more than 20,000,000 tons worth £715,000,000 were exported. With stocks rapidly diminishing action was urgently required and in 1909 a system of annual 'cropping' was instigated.

The colonies are flourishing and new ones have also been established on predator-free headlands on the mainland. The main danger seems to be that man's overfishing of the area will reduce the colonies, which must surely rank as one of the seven wonders of the avian world.

Off south-west Africa there are other guano islands. Here the important species are the Cape Cormorant (*P. capensis*), the Cape Gannet (*Sula capensis*) and the Black-footed Penguin. Once again after careless over-exploitation the guano industry is on a balanced 'cropping' basis.

Locations of guano producing areas

Cape Cormorant (left) and
Guanay Cormorant

In Asia man has also exploited cormorants, though for a completely different purpose – that of catching fish. Two species have been used, the Common Cormorant and the Japanese Cormorant (*P. capillatus*), both in Japan and China and in India. The latter species is usually caught by using bird-lime and decoys on the rocks which the cormorants have used for roosting during the winter months. In other instances the birds may be specially bred for the purpose and sold, normally untrained, to fishermen. The colonies from which the birds are taken receive special protection, and there are instances of this going back over hundreds of years.

The cormorants are trained to fish with a leather collar around their necks. This prevents them swallowing the catch and is also a convenient place to attach the line by which they are held. Training may take only a few weeks before the birds become most proficient.

In Japan the art dates back to at least the sixth century AD, and there are records of the catches sent to the Emperor dating back to AD 900. Fishing takes place on the Nagono river where certain sections have been set aside for this purpose. The season is from May 11th to October 15th and fishing is carried out except when the moon is full. Now the custom is a major tourist attraction rather than a means of providing food.

Japanese fishermen using cormorants to catch fish for them

The fishing is carried out at night from boats, each carrying a large flare at the stern which attracts the fish to the vicinity. Each boat has a crew of four, one of whom is known as the Usho or Cormorant Master and has twelve birds in his charge. Another, known as Uzukai, has control of four birds, the other members having responsibility for the boat and for the flare. The birds are removed from their baskets in a certain order beginning with the youngest, and once in the water quickly start to hunt the fish lured to the area. The birds swallow the fish as far as the collar and are then gently pulled back on board and the catch removed. If fish are plentiful as many as fifty may be caught by a well-trained bird in one night.

In China the art seems to date from at least the Sung dynasty (AD 960-1298), fishing being carried out by day from rafts moored on the rivers. Birds were often bred in captivity rather than being taken wild from colonies. With the advent of modern fishing methods the old custom is dying out.

As a sport the method flourished briefly in Great Britain under the Stuart kings, and the post of Master of the Cormorants was created. The birds were kept on ponds near the present site of the Houses of Parliament.

One species of cormorant is unique: the large Flightless Cormorant (*Nannopterum harrisi*) of the Galapagos Islands. It is about 90 cm (3 ft) in length and its brownish plumage, with paler underparts, is short and dense like that of a penguin. The wings are much reduced in size, the flight feathers in particular being reduced in number as well as size. Indeed, its wings are smaller in comparison with overall size than those of the extinct Great Auk (see pages 136 to 137). It is an expert swimmer, though when diving only the powerful webbed feet are used for propulsion, the wings remaining folded.

The Flightless Cormorant is an excellent example of a bird living in an isolated area, with an adequate all-year-round food supply and no natural predators, losing the powers of flight when no longer required. Even within the Galapagos Islands the bird's range is restricted to Albermarle and Narborough, while most are concentrated in the shallow-water strait between the two islands. The population is small. In 1961 it was considered to contain about 500 pairs, a fact which causes some concern, though at the present time the numbers show no sign of a decline.

Birds breed in all months of the year but the peak time seems to be from April to June, a period when the Humboldt current extends northwards and no doubt influences the food supply favourably. Prior to nest building and during it there is much display from both sexes; this usually takes the form of water dances. The birds swim about and as they pass bend their necks into an 'S' curve. At a later stage the male will lead the female ashore to a prospective nest site often encouraging her with low growls. Nests are bulky, constructed from seaweed torn from the rocks. The male collects the material while the female remains on guard and carries out the construction.

Three eggs seem to be the usual clutch and both parents take part in the incubation, the precise period of which is as yet unknown. Usually a single youngster only is reared as some eggs fail to hatch and many small chicks die. One parent always remains on guard at the nest site with the chick which is fed on fish and octopus. The fledging period is not known, but on leaving the nest chicks are fed for a while on the sea.

Flightless Cormorant of the Galapagos Islands

Several species of cormorant are found in the Antarctic and sub-Antarctic regions. They are often called shags in their breeding areas, perhaps from the long, shaggy plumes which several species grow – and quickly shed – during the breeding season. In Britain this name is restricted to the Green Cormorant, to distinguish it from the Common or Great Cormorant, the only other native species.

The Magellan Cormorant (*P. magellanicus*) is found, as its name suggests, in the Straits of Magellan and on the islands round Cape Horn. It extends northwards along the southern coasts of Patagonia and Chile and also occurs in the Falkland Islands. This species may be distinguished from the similar Blue-eyed Cormorant (*P. atriceps*) by its red face and the fact that its throat is feathered, while in the breeding season it has a white neck. Some authorities consider that the Magellan Cormorant is just a subspecies of the Blue-eyed. The latter breeds in much the same area, though it extends further north by several hundred miles. It is also found nesting well to the south on islands off Grahamland, in South Georgia, the South Orkneys and Shetlands and in the South Sandwich group.

The King Cormorant (*P. albiventer*) is similar in size and appearance to the last species, from which it can be distinguished by the extensions of purple-black plumage to the bill area and the absence of a white back patch. This species also breeds on the coasts of Patagonia and in the Falkland Islands, while further east it occurs in two subspecies on Crozet Island and Macquarie Island.

Blue-eyed Cormorant

Rough-faced
Cormorant (left),
Kerguelen
Cormorant
(centre) and King
Cormorant

The Kerguelen Cormorant (*P. verrucosus*) is found nesting only on Kerguelen Island.

On South Island in New Zealand and on the sub-Antarctic islands further south the Rough-legged Cormorant (*P. carunculatus*) occurs, together with some five subspecies, or perhaps only insular races, which can be recognized by the colour of the face and caruncles at the base of the bill.

Several species of cormorant are found more in the great river systems of the world than on the sea coasts, while others like the Double-crested Cormorant (*P. auritus*) frequent both habitats and may be found on coasts, rivers and inland lakes.

Reed Cormorant

All four species in the genus *Haliëtor* may be found on inland waters as well as the Indian Cormorant (*P. fuscicollis*), which is also found in Ceylon and Burma, and the Little Black Cormorant (*P. sulcirostris*) of the Malay archipelago and Australasia.

The Pigmy Cormorant is rarely seen on the coast. Its range extends from south-east Europe eastwards through Turkey and Persia as far as Afghanistan. Breeding colonies of this rather shy species may be quite large and are found among low bushes or in reed-beds. Quite often they will include other species like herons and egrets. The Pigmy Cormorant is a very handsome species with glossy green plumage heavily spotted with white, while in summer its head is a dark red-brown. Although rather clumsy on land the birds are most dextrous as they clamber about the vegetation. A frequent mode of perching is to use a vertical stem and sit, literally 'on their tails', which are hard pressed against the stem for support.

The Reed Cormorant or Long-tailed Shag (*H. africanus*) is found northwards from the Cape of Good Hope to Gambia and the Sudan, with a subspecies on Madagascar. A bird of rather solitary habits, it swims lower in the water than other species.

The Javanese or Little Cormorant (*H. niger*) is found throughout India, Burma, Ceylon, the Malay Peninsula and islands to Borneo. It may be distinguished from the Indian Cormorant by its smaller size, short bill and relatively long tail.

The Little Pied Cormorant (*H. melanoleucus*) is found on many of the Indonesian islands, New Guinea, Australia, Tasmania, New Zealand and New Caledonia. In a number of these areas subspecies have been described. Except for the New Zealand race, the underparts are white, and birds can be distinguished from other white-breasted species by the short bill and neck and long tail.

The Shag or Green Cormorant nests along rocky coasts from the White Sea and Iceland southwards to Morocco. It is also found in the Mediterranean and Aegean Seas and on the Crimean coast of the Black Sea. Strictly a bird of open coastlines, the Shag rarely enters far into estuaries and comes inland only when storm-driven. When diving for food it stays below for about a minute, though dives of a longer duration

Pigmy Cormorant (left) and Indian Cormorant

Adult Shag and chick

have been recorded. It is interesting to note the difference in the fish taken by the Shag and the Common Cormorant. The former takes a large proportion of sand eels while the latter takes quite a quantity of flat fish; indeed, half of its diet is said to be of marketable value.

With glossy green plumage, only offset by the yellow mouthparts, the Shag is a most handsome bird. Early in the breeding season its head is adorned with a forward-curving crest, though this quickly disappears as the season proceeds. Colonies of this species may be quite large like those of other cormorants, but in many instances pairs nest individually or in small groups. Typical sites are among boulders on scree slopes, on cliff ledges and in the dark recesses of sea caves.

Nests are large, bulky structures of seaweed and vegetation taken from close at hand, while any suitable piece of flotsam may also be added, a child's plastic tractor being found on one occasion. The normal clutch seems to be three eggs, though up to six have been recorded. Incubation, which is carried out by both parents, is not by the conventional brood-patch for this is absent in the cormorants. Instead, the heat of the large webbed feet is used, the bird shuffling them beneath the eggs when settling on the nest. The incubation period is from thirty to thirty-four days; on hatching the chicks are jet-black, blind, naked and helpless.

Chicks are fed on regurgitated fish and soon become covered in brownish down, this finally being replaced by brown feathers which are paler underneath. Fledging takes place during the seventh week, though some chicks are looked after by their parents for up to a further seven weeks. During this time the birds collect in large numbers on favourite rocks. Later, when dispersal takes place, some individuals roam several hundred miles from the colony, though adults seem much more sedentary.

The Shag, at least in Great Britain, has been increasing in numbers during recent years. This has been particularly marked in north-east England and south-east Scotland. Although changes in the available food supply have been suggested as the reason for this, it seems much more likely to be due to the cessation of human persecution.

(Top to bottom) Young Shags in second winter and summer, first winter and summer, and juvenile plumage

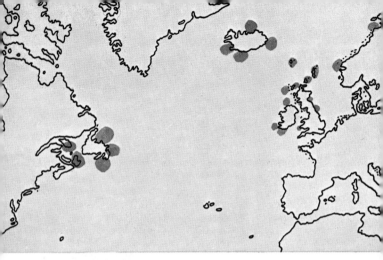

Distribution of North Atlantic Gannet

Gannets

The headquarters of the North Atlantic Gannet (*Sula bassana*) are undoubtedly the colonies round Great Britain and Ireland, the largest being those on the great stacks of St Kilda where gannets have nested for 1,000 years or more; 44,529 pairs nested in 1959. The colony on the Bass Rock was first noted as flourishing in 1521, while the first reference to those on Ailsa Craig was in 1527. The colony on Sula Sgeir was noted in 1549

North Atlantic Gannet

North Atlantic Gannet diving and in flight

and that on Sula Stack in 1710. The colonies on Shetland were founded during the early years of the present century; 6,000 pairs were nesting on Noss by 1959 and, in 1965, between 4,000 and 5,000 on Hermaness. The most recent colony to be established is that on the Scar Rocks, Wigtownshire, in 1939; in 1968 it contained 437 nests.

In England the only colony to be established was on Bempton Cliffs, Yorkshire, in 1937. In 1965 it contained fourteen pairs. A once thriving colony on Lundy Island in the Bristol Channel became extinct during the nineteenth century, at the same time as one was becoming established on Grassholme off the south-west coast of Wales. In 1964 this contained 15,528 pairs.

There are three colonies in Ireland: Great Saltee, Co. Wexford contained 150 pairs in 1968; the number of pairs at Bull Rock, Co. Cork had risen to 500 in 1955; while in 1966 there were 17,700 pairs nesting on the Little Skellig, Co. Kerry, the second largest colony in the world.

Elsewhere in the North Atlantic, colonies have been founded in recent years in Norway, the Channel Islands and off Brittany. Others, sometimes large, whose early history is often obscure are known from the Faroes, Newfoundland, Canada and Iceland.

As we have seen in the preceding pages gannets resort to large densely packed colonies for breeding. Each nest is placed just beyond the reach of its neighbours, but no further. It is generally made from seaweed and grass, a bulky structure which may be as much as 60 cm (2 ft) high with sloping slides and a hollow for the single egg. Such nests are necessary to keep the egg or chick out of the guano slime which forms the nest site of the colony.

A single egg is laid, usually during April. Like the cormorants the gannets have no brood-patch, incubation in this case being carried out by the birds placing their webbed feet, slightly overlapping, on the egg. This takes some forty-two days to hatch, both sexes sharing the incubation. The chick takes about thirty-six hours to emerge from the time the chipping commences. During this time the egg is removed to rest on the upper surface of the parent's feet.

Weighing some 60 gm when hatched, the chick will increase to a maximum weight of about 4,500 gm by the time it is nine weeks old. During the first two weeks chicks are brooded by one or other parent, and even after this period one will remain on guard while the other is away fishing. Food is brought back in the throat of the adult, from which it is removed by the chick forcing its own bill deep inside. The first growth of down is white, but this is eventually replaced by mottled brown feathers, adult plumage not being attained until the

Breeding areas and movements of North Atlantic Gannets

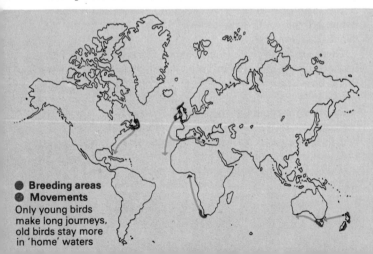

● **Breeding areas**
◐ **Movements**
Only young birds
make long journeys,
old birds stay more
in 'home' waters

Sweeping bows to one another

Aggression between two adults

Chick 'bill hiding' at
the approach of an adult

Friendly ceremony performed
when birds meet at nesting site

Chick pestering adult

Adult feeding chick

Display postures of North Atlantic Gannets

fourth year of life when the young birds begin to breed.

Chicks that are on the edge of a colony leave the nest in comparative comfort, but others may have to stagger many yards, set about on all sides by angry adults whose nests they pass. The first flight may, if conditions are right, last for several miles. The chick is now alone, though with ample fat reserves it need not feed for up to three weeks. During this time it must learn to fish and fly, a stage of its life which may never be properly observed by man.

Young gannets are great wanderers. Many in the first years of life go south to spend their time off the coasts of West Africa. Later they will remain more in home waters, the colonies being deserted only during the brief mid-winter months.

Two other species of gannet, the Cape Gannet or Malgash (*S. capensis*) and the Australian Gannet (*S. serrator*), are found in the southern hemisphere, but differences from the northern species are slight.

The Cape Gannet nests on a scattering of islands off South Africa, where all the colonies are strictly protected. Aerial means have been used to effect accurate surveys of the population, which is considered to be about 500,000 pairs. Unlike most North Atlantic colonies, those of the Cape Gannet tend to be on fairly flat, low islands. The eggs are laid in October and the incubation and fledging periods are similar to those of the northern species.

Large numbers of Cape Gannet chicks have been ringed, and again it has been found that it is the juveniles which wander most. Many move north to the Gulf of Guinea in the first months of life, though later they return to home waters and become more sedentary.

The Cape Gannet along with the Cape Cormorant and Black-footed Penguin is an important guano producer. It is said that gannets nesting on the same islands as the penguins leave passages through their colonies in order to give the penguins easy access to and from the sea.

Cape Gannet

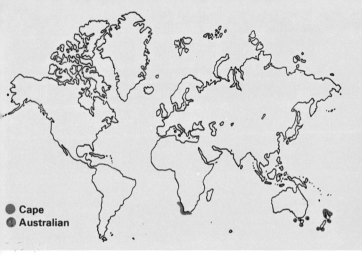

● Cape
◑ Australian

The Australian Gannet breeds on islands in the Bass Strait and off Tasmania, while others are found off North Island, New Zealand. It has a much smaller population than its relatives, in the early 1950s being estimated at about 21,000 pairs. Again ringing has shown that most movement takes place during the first years of life, with New Zealand birds travelling eastwards to Australian waters.

(Above) Distribution of Cape and Australian Gannets

Boobies

The six species of booby are found throughout the warm oceans of the world. Included in the same family as the gannets they are similar in many respects to them. For example, they use the same plunge-diving mode of catching prey, though with adaptations. The Brown Booby (*S. leucogaster*) makes more shallow, angled dives while the Red-footed Booby (*S. sula*) will take flying fish, besides squid which it catches on the surface at night.

The Red-footed Booby is found on many islands in the Caribbean, South Atlantic, Indian and Pacific Oceans, including the Galapagos Islands where an enormous colony of some 140,000 pairs nests on Tower Island. It is one of two booby species which nest in trees and bushes, sometimes at a con-

Brown Booby (top) and
Masked Booby

siderable height above the ground. The single egg takes some forty-six days to hatch. The chick, like those of other members of the family, is quite helpless at first and is brooded by one or other parent until it is some six weeks old. The fledging period seems to vary somewhat between different breeding sites from as little as fourteen weeks up to nineteen weeks. Though able to fly, the chicks continue to return to their nest sites to be fed for up to a further fifteen weeks.

The Brown Booby is also found in the Caribbean, tropical Atlantic and Indian Oceans. At Ascension Island, where it has received particular attention, pairs stay at the nest site throughout the year and can therefore commence breeding very quickly when the food supply reaches an adequate level. If food becomes short, growing chicks can starve for a considerable period, their growth slowing or stopping entirely.

Red-footed Booby

The Blue-footed Booby (*S. nebouxii*) is the largest species, being some 86 cm (34 in) in length. It nests on a scattering of islands from Mexico south to Ecuador and Peru, and its two, occasionally three, eggs take about forty-one days to hatch. Chicks fledge by about the fourteenth week and are cared for by their parents for a further period of up to seven weeks. The birds are at least partially nocturnal in that they may bring food in to the colony during the hours of darkness, though whether this is actually caught at night is not known.

Abbot's Booby only nests, often in trees and bushes, on Christmas Island in the Indian Ocean, where the most recent estimate of its population is 2,000 pairs.

The Peruvian Booby (*S. variegata*) or 'piquero' breeds only on islands off Peru where it occurs in vast colonies, one being estimated in 1964 to contain 356,340 pairs, while the total population must run into many millions. This is a species which together with the Guanay Cormorant is a most efficient guano producer. Indeed, its nest is no more than a bowl of droppings into which a few feathers are incorporated as they fall, and sometimes an occasional piece of seaweed.

The clutch consists of three, sometimes four, eggs which take about forty-three days to hatch. The chicks are guarded

Peruvian Booby

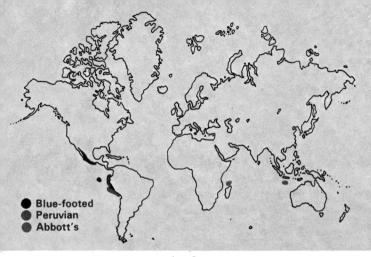

● **Blue-footed**
● **Peruvian**
● **Abbott's**

Distribution of Blue-footed, Peruvian and Abbot's Boobies

throughout the fledging period by one or other parent, quite unlike the other boobies where the chicks are left after a time while the parents search for food. The fledging period is thought to be about fourteen weeks, though the chicks are not independent for some time after this.

Blue-footed Booby (front) and Abbot's Booby

From time to time the vast seabird colonies off Peru suffer what seem to be catastrophic crashes in numbers. The cool, food-rich currents are pushed back south by warmer waters from the north – the El Nino. This quickly affects the food supply and hundreds of thousands of birds die, chicks starve to death and eggs remain unincubated. However, once the current systems revert to normal, the super-abundant food supply is re-established and the colonies recoup their losses at an almost staggering rate.

Pelicans

Pelicans belong to a single genus and opinions differ among ornithologists as to whether there are six, seven or eight species. This is due to the number of subspecies which have been described. They are found in many parts of the world, mainly in tropical regions but also in more temperate zones. The range of some species is discontinuous. For instance, the Eastern White Pelican (*Pelecanus onocrotalus*) is to be found on a number of lakes and rivers in south-eastern Europe, the Middle East, Asiatic Russia and Africa south to the Cape. Quite often many hundreds of miles will separate one breeding area from another. Some species are more birds of estuaries, rivers and inland lakes, while others are strictly maritime in their habits.

They are all large birds, the Dalmatian Pelican (*P. crispus*) being 182 cm (6 ft) in length, while the Brown Pelican (*P. occidentalis*), the smallest, is some 122 cm (4 ft). Through being widely kept in zoos and through their appearances in cartoons and advertisements, the pelicans are well known. The long beak complete with large extendible gular pouch is of special note. This is used much as a net for catching fish which are promptly swallowed; it is not a storage organ, despite its reputed ability to hold 'enough food for a week'!

Although pelicans seem ungainly on land and their take-off from water is a laborious affair, once airborne they are magnificent. Flying in long lines with necks retracted they may under favourable circumstances achieve quite an altitude.

(Top to bottom) Dalmatian Pelican, Australian Pelican and American White Pelican

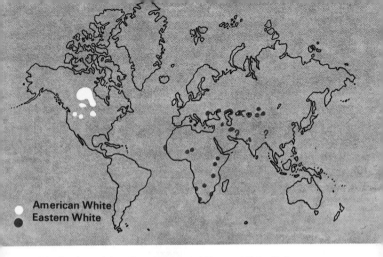

American White
Eastern White

Distribution of American White and Eastern White Pelicans

Several species are migratory, at least in parts of their range. The American White Pelican (*P. erythrorhynchos*) nests from western Canada south to Texas. Its autumn migration takes it south-east to the Gulf of Mexico and the Caribbean area. The Eastern White Pelican leaves the north of its breeding area in winter and moves south to the Persian Gulf, India and the Malay Peninsula.

Pelicans are often communal in their feeding. Birds will form into lines in order to drive fish in towards shallow water by beating their wings on the surface. The Brown Pelican dives for food like the gannets; while doing so it keeps its neck retracted as during flight. The food requirements of such large birds are prodigious. It is considered that an Eastern White Pelican will eat ten per cent of its body weight in fish per day, i.e. between 900 and 1,200 gm. If this is the case the colony at Lake Rukwa with 40,000 pairs, the largest in Africa, would consume 17,000 tons of fish in a year.

Pelican colonies are usually large, noisy and smelly avian metropolises. Nests are bulky affairs of sticks placed in bushes and trees, as in the case of the Pink-backed Pelican (*P. rufescens*), or on the ground, often among reeds, as in the Eastern White Pelican. The main objective is for the site to be free from predatory animals, which in Africa include the Hyaena and Jackal, while even a Lion will make a meal of an unwary pelican. Unusual sites include some in walled towns, like Kano in northern Nigeria, and on inaccessible cliffs and crags sometimes far from water.

Up to four eggs are laid, usually pale blue in colour. Both parents take turns with the incubation, the period of which depends on the species and seems to vary between thirty and forty days. Chicks are helpless and naked at first and are brooded continuously through these stages. Later the parents just stand over them to afford some shade from the sun. The chicks are fed on partially digested fish which they obtain by thrusting their own head deep into the parent's throat.

In ground-nesting pelicans the first four weeks or so in a chick's life seem to be spent in the nest area, after which they form into groups or 'pods'. These may be very large, but even so chicks are fed by their own parents and indeed will seek them out in order to receive a meal. Fledging seems to be accomplished at about the tenth week.

Grey (top) and Pink-backed Pelicans

The Brown Pelican is a bird of the New World, occurring in a number of subspecies from California in the west and South Carolina in the east southwards through the Caribbean zone to South America. On the east coast it does not extend further south than the delta of the Orinoco. In the west the coasts of Ecuador, Peru and Chile, including oceanic islands like the Galapagos, are frequented by this bird. The Chilean race is considered by some to be a separate species as it is a much larger bird than its northern relatives, being up to 182 cm (6 ft) in length compared with 122 cm (4 ft).

Depending on the area, nests may be found either in trees – mangrove swamps being a favourite spot – or on the ground. If in a tree, then a rough platform of large twigs is constructed, while on the ground a scrape with some feathers as lining suffices. Nests are often packed densely together with only enough room between each to ensure that physical contact

Chilean (top) and Brown Pelican

Distribution of Chilean and Brown Pelicans

• **Brown**
• **Chilean**

between the incubating birds is avoided.

The courtship activities of the Brown Pelican have been described as a most sombre affair with all the solemnity of a funeral. The male circles the squatting female, lifting his wings and stretching his neck, all in silence. Finally the female flies out to sea, followed by the male, and it is on the water that mating takes place.

The nesting season is somewhat irregular, varying from site to site and at the same site each year to year. Three eggs are generally laid and both parents take part in the incubation which takes some twenty-eight days. As with other species the chicks are naked and helpless at first, but with the rich fish food grow rapidly. They have a piercing scream as a food call. Those on the ground roam about a good deal after several weeks in the nest, while those in trees are much more restricted. They are able to climb down when they are seven weeks old, though before then many will have fallen to their death. Mortality among tree-nesters must be high.

The Chilean subspecies is one of the guano birds, others being mentioned on pages 28 to 29, 72 to 73 and 92 to 93. It is not nearly so numerous as the other species, among which it nests. By virtue of its large size, however, it finds no difficulty in acquiring a nest site among the teeming multitudes.

Skuas

The skuas, or jaegers as they are known in the New World, are a small family – the Stercorariidae – closely allied to the gulls. Four species are found in the northern hemispheres, one of which, the Great Skua (*Catharacta skua*), also occurs in the polar zones of the southern hemisphere. It is widely distributed

Great Skua chasing a Kittiwake

in this area, with a number of sub-species from Chile eastwards along the edge of the Antarctic continent and its islands to New Zealand.

The Great Skua, a heavily built bird about 58 cm (23 in) in length, may easily be distinguished from brown immature gulls by its build and the prominent white wing-patches which are visible during flight. It is more of a scavenger than the other species, frequently following ships and fishing fleets. It will also kill both chicks and adult birds of smaller species besides being a great egg-stealer. Indeed, in the south nests are often situated close to penguin colonies which afford an easy food supply.

In Great Britain there has been a marked increase in this species during the last fifty years or so. For a time in the last century it was restricted to Foula, its main stronghold, and Unst, Shetland. However, since about 1920 it has increased in numbers and has spread south, now nesting elsewhere in Shetland, in the Orkney Islands, Caithness, Sutherland and the Outer Hebrides including St Kilda. It has been suggested that during this expansion the Iceland population has decreased, so that there has been a shift in the breeding range towards the south rather than an overall increase in numbers.

Of the other species the Pomarine Skua or Jaeger (*Stercorarius pomarinus*) is the largest, being some 53 cm (21 in) in length, and may be distinguished by its size, larger bill and curiously twisted central tail feathers. It nests on the tundras of northern Siberia, various Arctic islands, Greenland, northern Canada and Alaska.

The smallest species, the Long-tailed Skua or Jaeger (*S. longicaudus*), has the central tail feathers extending up to a further 20 cm (8 in), making a total length of 50 cm (20 in). Its breeding range is circumpolar, extending further north than any other skua, though coming far south in some regions. It is a thinly scattered species throughout its whole range and for successful breeding seems dependent on lemmings, its chief source of food.

The Arctic Skua or Parasitic Jaeger (*S. parasiticus*) is perhaps the most common skua species. It breeds along the coasts and islands of the polar basin, extending southwards through Norway and Sweden, and in Great Britain, where it has in-

creased during the present century and is now widespread in Shetland, Orkney and the Outer Hebrides. It is found in Caithness on the mainland of Scotland, and also on certain islands in the south Inner Hebrides like Coll and Jura. Occasionally birds spend the summer in western Ireland, though there are no breeding records as yet.

As its name suggests, this species is dependent to a considerable extent on others for food. This it obtains by harrying, though rarely coming into actual physical contact with, species like terns and gulls. After sometimes only the briefest of chases, the victim will drop or disgorge its food and continue unmolested while the skua swoops down to feed.

In the three species of *Stercorarius* polymorphism occurs, though only rarely in the Long-tailed Skua. Polymorphism is the term used to describe the fact 'that in a single interbreeding population, two or more readily distinguishable and

Arctic Skua, light (left), dark (centre) and intermediate colour phases

genetically determined forms – called morphs – occur', too great in number to be explained by recurrent mutation.

In the Arctic Skua both dark and light phases occur, together with intermediates, and these have received particular attention through the counting of the phases throughout the bird's range. Although the phases readily interbreed there is a tendency for birds to mate with those of the same type rather than of the opposite. For instance Richard Perry, making observations on Noss, Shetland, noted that twenty-one matings were between dark pairs, seven between light pairs and nine were mixed matings. Similar observations have also been made at other colonies.

In Shetland recent work by L.S.V. and U. M. Venables estimated that between twenty-five and thirty per cent of the population were pale phase in the islands. This ratio increases as one moves northwards through the bird's range.

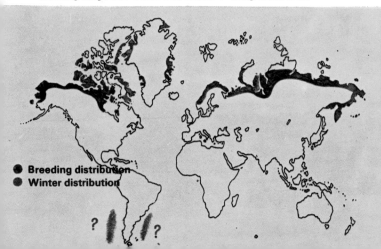

Long-tailed Skua

Skuas breed either in loose colonies or individually, usually on bleak moorland and tundras. Some colonies may be very large, for instance that of the Great Skua on Foula contains about 900 pairs. The nest is a depression in the ground or vegetation, lined with dry grass and the occasional feather.

The two or three eggs take about twenty-three days to hatch in the case of the Long-tailed Skua and twenty-eight days for the Great Skua. Both parents take a share in the incubation, the off-duty bird often standing guard close by. Any intruder in the nesting area is mobbed and chased with vigour, including man himself.

The chicks, which are covered at first with a warm brown down, are quite active and within several days leave the nest to hide close by. During the breeding season Arctic Skuas will often try to lure one away from the nest area by means of a distraction display, flapping about on the ground nearby as

Breeding range and winter distribution of Long-tailed Skua

Breeding distribution
Winter distribution

if injured. The chicks are able to fly by the time they are about seven weeks old, but for a further two weeks or so they may remain dependent on their parents for support.

Skuas are great wanderers during the off-season. The southern race of the Great Skua comes north into tropical waters, some crossing the Equator to appear off Japan and British Columbia, while one ringed in the South Shetlands was recovered in the French West Indies. The northern race seems to frequent the North Atlantic; it was thought not to go beyond the Tropic of Capricorn, though the recent recovery of a Foula-ringed bird from Guyana seems to alter this idea.

Arctic Skuas certainly have a trans-equatorial migration with recoveries of ringed birds being reported from either shore of the South Atlantic. Long-tailed Skuas also move south to that area and are reported from South American waters in particular.

Pomarine Skua

Breeding range and winter distribution of Pomarine Skua

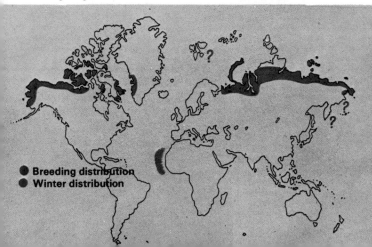

● Breeding distribution
● Winter distribution

Gulls

Gulls must be about the most familiar of all seabirds, though many species are hardly seabirds at all. They spend much of their life inland. Some species may breed inland and winter on the coast. Saunders' Gull (*Larus saundersi*) nests on lakes in Mongolia but winters on the coast of Korea and China. Others like the Kittiwake (*Rissa tridactyla*) are much more maritime.

The forty-four or so species are distributed throughout the world, from the high Arctic to the snowy fastness of Antarc-

Ring-billed Gull

tica. Some are widespread; the Common Gull (*L. canus*), for instance, nests in a range that extends across much of northern Europe, Asia and Canada. Others, like Audouin's Gull of the Mediterranean (see pages 12 to 13) and the Swallow-tailed Gull (*Creagrus furcatus*) of the Galapagos, are very restricted in their range.

Gulls are generally noisy species, especially at nesting colonies, where the slightest disturbance will unleash a sound which is almost deafening. In size the species range from the Greater Black-backed Gull (*L. marinus*), a majestic bird some 76 cm (30 in) in length, to the Little Gull (*L. minutus*), a bare 25 cm (10 in). All species are stoutly built with long wings and short tails. They are excellent flyers and take every advantage of updraughts and eddies in order to effect flight with the minimum of effort. They will glide almost motionless in the slipstream of a ship or circle high in a thermal while flying home to roost.

Gulls may be divided into three distinct groups: the large white-headed gulls, a typical representative being the Ring-billed Gull (*L. delawarensis*) which breeds on lakes in Canada and the north-western United States; the hooded gulls, which include all those species with a dark head and of which the Sabine's Gull (*Xema sabini*) is a northern example; the Ivory Gull (*Pagophila eburnea*), the only all-white gull, is the solitary representative in its group. It breeds on islands never far from the Arctic pack ice, and is only a rare straggler further south; even in the Polar winter it does not stray far beyond the ice limit.

Ivory Gull

Gulls are chiefly colonial nesters. Some colonies are very large, like that on Walney Island, England which in 1969 contained some 17,500 pairs of Lesser Black-backed Gulls and 17,000 pairs of Herring Gulls. Other species may also nest in colonies, though at times they are more scattered. Nest sites vary a good deal with the habitat. Most are on the ground, but Bonaparte's Gull (*L. philadelphia*) may use a tree site. Nests may be placed in tussocks of grass or among floating vegetation, other sites may be on cliff ledges or in sand dunes, while buildings are by no means disdained.

Nests are composed of dry vegetation, feathers, small bones and other debris found close at hand. Quite a bulky structure may be the result, and in some cases the same site may be used, with additions, for several seasons. Two or three eggs are laid and these are normally brown or green in colour, blotched and

Young Great Black-backed Gull in second winter plumage (top) and juvenile

Adult Great Black-backed Gull and chick

speckled with darker markings. Both sexes take part in the incubation which, depending on the species, takes up to four weeks. Should the clutch be lost during the early stages the bird will lay again after an interval, sometimes using the same nest or perhaps moving to a completely new one. If during the actual laying period an egg is removed this will be replaced several times, even, it is said, up to fifteen times.

The chicks on hatching are covered with speckled brown down and leave the nest within a day or so. They are particularly difficult to find as their 'camouflage' makes them almost invisible. They lose the down within several weeks, and in their juvenile plumage look rather bedraggled and ugly. The precise fledging time is often difficult to assess because the young hide or, if disturbed, move well away from the nest site. However, from a number of species that have been studied it seems to be about seven weeks. Young gulls do not mature for several years and in the case of the Greater Black-backed Gull, four years elapse before full adult plumage is attained.

The Kittiwake and Red-legged Kittiwake (*Rissa brevirostris*) are among the most maritime of gulls. The former nests on sea cliffs along many coasts in northern Europe, Asia and North America, while the latter is restricted to islands in the Bering Sea.

Both species are maritime in their habits, only coming ashore to nest and spending the off-season roaming the northern oceans. The Kittiwake, as indicated by many recoveries of birds ringed in Great Britain, habitually crosses the North Atlantic to be found off eastern Canada and along the west coast of Greenland.

Kittiwakes normally nest on steep cliffs, where their rather large nests seem to adhere to the smallest ledges and rock niches. Occasionally there are records of birds nesting in areas of sand dunes and even on top of a discarded oil drum, but the most significant change seems to have taken place within recent years in Great Britain. Here the number of birds has increased quite remarkably with many new colonies being established. Low and more accessible cliffs are now being used together with such artificial sites as harbour walls, a seaside pier and a warehouse. The latter site is at Dunbar, Scotland, where the colony nesting on the window ledges must be about the easiest of all seabird colonies to count!

Besides this move to more man-made sites, birds have moved inland for several miles to nest on riverside buildings on the Tyne, a heavily polluted and industrialized river. Birds in the same area have been observed feeding on bread and scraps being thrown to other species. These developments would seem to indicate that a marked change is possible in the habits of the Kittiwake, though whether this will occur is certainly an open question.

Nesting in confined situations, the Kittiwake does show several adaptations to its environment. The normal clutch size is two as a larger number of chicks would not be possible in the confined space. The chicks remain almost stationary on the nest, and if the nest is on level ground they do not leave to take shelter, as do the chicks of other gull species when danger threatens.

Kittiwake and chicks (nest on warehouse window-ledge)

The Herring Gull has been the subject of much research. In 1937 F. Goethe published the results of his studies on the courtship, display and nesting of this species. This early work has been expanded by other workers, notably K. Paludan in Sweden and Professor Niko Tinbergen first in Holland and then in Great Britain. Some of the results of the latter's work have been published in *The Herring Gull's World*, a classic account of avian behaviour.

In many areas adult Herring Gulls are mainly sedentary, travelling each day from their roost on or near the colony to a feeding area which may be only a few miles away. As the weather gets warmer during the early spring, the birds will remain longer at the colony and the males begin to take up their territories. As these are only used for nesting and not as a feeding area, the piece of ground occupied may be quite small. The females are gradually attracted in, and as the same pieces of ground may be occupied for a period of years it often happens that the same pairs are formed. This probably occurs in many other seabird species. Experiments have shown that Herring Gulls are quite able to recognize their mates at thirty yards but are unable to recognize their eggs. Indeed they will sit on anything that is even only an approximation of the size and shape of an egg!

The territory is guarded from all intruders by the holder's use of various displays and threat postures. Although the colony may be divided up quite haphazardly into territories, by the time the eggs are laid each bird knows its neighbours and the limits of its own area, and intruders are rapidly driven off. Chicks which remain in their territory are relatively safe, those that stray are generally killed by neighbouring adults.

Much interesting work using model bills has been done with chicks. It has been shown conclusively that the red spot near the tip of an adult's yellow bill acts as a stimulus to the chicks to beg for food. Little reaction is evoked by a bill where this spot has been erased. The fact that the chicks beg for food on catching sight of the red bill also promotes the reaction in the adults of feeding them.

Chick pecking at artificial beak

Various experiments were carried out in order to see how recognition is achieved and in this a number of model eggs and shells were used. It was found that the factors which lead to shell removal are that a broken shell has a thin, serrated edge and shows white inside, whereas a whole egg has no edge, a smooth outline and shows no white, being brown with black markings. In addition an egg-shell is tested for weight, and should this be well above that of an empty shell the impulse to remove it will be checked. This act prevents chicks which have hatched but not yet completely left the shell being carried away in error.

Selecting discarded egg-shells from unhatched and hatching eggs

The Black-headed Gull (*L. ridibundus*), another widespread species, has also received a good deal of attention from ornithologists interested in bird behaviour. In 1937 Kirkman's *Bird Behaviour* was published, a book being based mainly on work upon this species.

In more recent years experiments and observations have been made by Professor Tinbergen and students at the Ravenglass Nature Reserve, Cumberland, England. Here in 1969 some 10,000 pairs nested.

One aspect studied is the method of egg-shell removal from the nest. It has been shown that an empty egg-shell placed close to an egg on the open beach means that the egg will be more vulnerable to predation by other gulls and the Carrion Crow. It would seem therefore that the removal of egg-shells from the vicinity of the nest is of particular importance in order to curtail the amount of predation on unhatched eggs or small chicks.

It has been observed that a gull will role an egg back into the nest, but will quickly remove a shell. What are the characteristics which enable shells to be distinguished from the unhatched egg? Six were listed, five of which were distinguishable by sight; the sixth was weight and could only be distinguished by actually moving the egg or shell.

In many parts of the world the numbers of gulls have increased dramatically, often to the detriment of other species, which in many cases are considered 'more attractive', and of man himself. Much of this increase seems attributable to the amount of waste material available, not only on rubbish dumps and in river systems but also discarded by fishing fleets at sea. Whether the gull population would decrease if all these alternative sources were removed is a debatable point. From the evidence so far available it seems that these highly adaptable birds would find other means of supply, and they are, of course, also capable of fishing for themselves.

The increase in gulls seems to have commenced in Britain during the latter half of the nineteenth century, when the first bird protection acts began to have an effect. At the same time the human populations of some remote islands were diminishing, and in certain cases even being evacuated completely; there was also less of a need to live quite so much off the land. Thus predation by man on seabird colonies decreased.

Studies have been made of several species of gull, and in each case the story is the same: that of an increase, often spectacular. Seventeen thousand pairs of Herring Gulls now nest on Walney Island where in 1947 there were only 120 pairs. The colony on the Isle of May, Scotland, established in 1907, contained 455 pairs in 1936, 3,000 in 1954 and 11,000 in 1967. The Black-headed Gull population of England and Wales increased by some twenty-five per cent between the years 1938 and 1958.

The Great Black-backed Gull in England and Wales was virtually extinct as a breeding species at the turn of the century. Since then its numbers have soared from 600-800 pairs in the 1930s to over 2,200 pairs at the present time. This is a species which has also increased quite dramatically along the eastern seaboard of the United States since the first breeding record in 1916.

It is a bird of particular menace to other species, especially to Manx Shearwaters and puffins. Indeed, at one Welsh colony the shearwater comprises some forty-five per cent of the gulls' food during the breeding season. This was a state of affairs that had to be checked, to some extent at least, by control measures. In this case a trapping campaign was started.

Food of Great Black-backed Gull

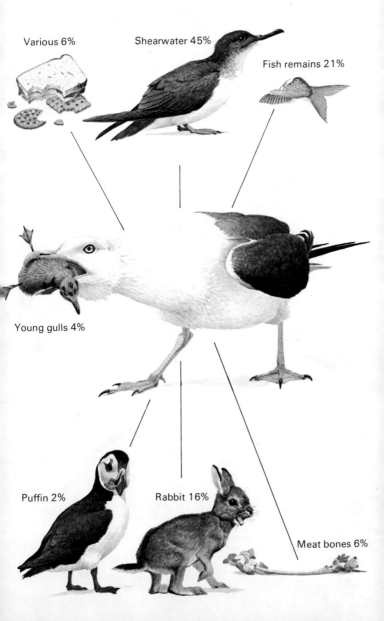

Various 6%

Shearwater 45%

Fish remains 21%

Young gulls 4%

Puffin 2%

Rabbit 16%

Meat bones 6%

The increase of gulls has brought about a number of problems, one of which, as we have just seen, is predation on smaller seabirds. The arrival of some species may literally swamp out others. This is of particular importance in the case of tern colonies which have suffered in some areas through the sudden expansion in gull numbers.

The Avocet colony at Havergate Island, Suffolk, a reserve of the Royal Society for the Protection of Birds, was threatened by Black-headed Gulls which were taking virtually all the season's production of chicks. The gulls were eventually driven off after their nests had been continually raked out; predation has now been greatly minimized. In the Camargue narcotic baits have been used with effect against predatory Herring Gulls, and in Holland a campaign using strychnine against the same species has had a limited effect in containing the population. Other methods have been tried, including sterilization of both adults and eggs. Gulls, being very long-lived species, require to produce very few chicks during their lifetime in order to keep a stable population. Any control, therefore, must of necessity be wide-ranging and efficient in order to have the desired effect.

Gulls are a particular nuisance at airfields at which they often congregate to feed or rest. This creates quite a problem as aircraft collisions with birds are most dangerous during take-off and landing. The annual cost to the Royal Air Force from damage received by this means is estimated to be about £1,000,000, and in Britain half of the strikes are by gulls.

It is possible to curtail the activities of gulls on airfields by means of the playing of alarm calls, while the Royal Navy has had success using falcons. Greater difficulties are encountered when gulls fly over an airfield on their way to and from a roost. Such flights are not so easily diverted.

Gulls habitually using reservoirs may pollute them with *Salmonella* picked up through feeding on rubbish dumps and at sewage outfalls. They may possibly transmit avian tuberculosis to cattle, and have been associated with the spread of bovine cysticercosis.

A new and growing habit is that of nesting on buildings,

Herring Gulls (top and centre) and Common Gulls (bottom)

particularly in coastal towns. They foul buildings and pavements, while the noise created is a considerable nuisance early in the morning. This seems to be a new menace which could create more serious problems than city pigeons or starlings.

Two species of gulls inhabit the high Arctic regions besides the Ivory Gull (see pages 106 to 107). These are Sabine's Gull (*Xema sabini*) and Ross's Gull (*Rhodosethia rosea*), both of which are interesting though little-known birds.

Sabine's Gull was first discovered by a member of John Ross's first Arctic expedition in 1818 on islands in Melville Bay, north-west Greenland. The discoverer, E. Sabine, also gave his name to the islands.

The Sabine's Gull is probably the most tern-like of all gulls, with a light, buoyant flight and a grating, tern-like cry. It breeds in marshy areas, often close to Arctic Tern colonies, in Alaska, Arctic Canada, Greenland and Arctic Siberia. The nest is a mere hollow lined with grass in which two or three eggs are laid. The winter range is imperfectly known. There seems to be a small autumn passage southwards off western

European coasts, but spring records are few.

Ross's Gull is a much rarer visitor to European waters. For instance, there are only a handful of records from Great Britain. Although first discovered by James Clark Ross, then a member of Parry's second expedition in search of the Northwest Passage in 1823, the next fifty years or so produced very few further records and no sign of a nesting site.

Explorers on board the ill-fated 'Jeanette', trapped in pack-ice north of Siberia, saw numbers of these birds and more skins were procured. Three were brought out by one of the survivors who carried them beneath his shirt across the pack ice after the ship was crushed in the floe. Other explorers amid the polar ice, including Nansen himself, encountered more birds. It was not until 1905, however, that a nest was found – by S. A. Buterlin in the delta of the Kolyma River in eastern Siberia. Although birds are seen in Alaska and northern Canada it seems as though the only nesting area is among the tussocks of rough grass on boggy moorland in the river valleys close to the tree-line of northern Siberia.

Terns

Like their close relatives the gulls, the terns or Sternidae are a large group of almost worldwide distribution, their main stronghold being the Pacific Basin. There are some thirty-nine species and many subspecies, one of the largest being the Crested Tern (*Sterna bernsteini*), some 53 cm (21 in) in length, which is common in the Indian Ocean and western Pacific. There are a number of very small species little more than 20 to 22 cm (8-9 in) in length, including the Damara Tern (*S.*

Roseate Tern in flight

balaenarum) of South African waters and the Amazon Tern (*S. superciliaris*) of South American river systems.

Terns are slender birds with long wings and forked tails, giving rise to the general name 'sea-swallows'. The bill is generally long and slender though in some species, notably the Gull-billed Tern (*Gelochelidon nilotica*), it is much more ponderous. Both the bill and legs may be brightly coloured, usually red, yellow or black, or a combination of these.

Fish and small invertebrates seem to be the main food; these

Roseate Tern on its nest

are caught by the birds swooping down, often plunging partly beneath the surface in order to effect a capture. While fishing they hold their heads down and hover in flight in a most characteristic manner. Although they have webbed feet terns only rarely swim or rest on the water, preferring to stand on a beach or a convenient floating object.

They may be divided broadly into three main groups. The black-capped terns containing over thirty species are found in all oceans and on many inland river and lake systems. The noddy terns comprise a group of five species found only in tropical regions: two are dark in colour, two intermediate and one mainly white. There is only a solitary representative in the last group, the Inca Tern (*Larosterna inca*), which is found on islands off the coasts of southern Peru and Chile.

When nesting, the terns are a very gregarious family and some colonies are of tremendous size. A colony of the Sooty Tern (*S. fuscata*) in the Seychelles was believed to contain 5,000,000 pairs some thirty years ago. A more recent survey on the same island gave the population as 1,210,000 pairs, which worked out at an average density of two and a half pairs per square metre (square yard), with over three pairs per square metre (square yard) in suitable places.

Fairy Tern and egg

Sooty Tern and chick (left) and Inca Tern at nest

Just as the species are varied in their breeding habits, so are the nesting sites which they use. Birds nesting on open shingle beaches or on sand dunes make do with the barest of scrapes. Some of the marsh terns construct nests of floating vegetation which may either float themselves or be placed on mounds of floating debris. The Common Noddy (*Anous stolidus*) builds untidy nests of seaweed in low bushes and shrubs. The White Noddy or Fairy Tern (*A. albus*) lays a single egg balanced on the branch of a tree or on a rock ledge. The chick is adapted for such a precarious existence in that it can hang upside down if necessary, keeping purchase with its claws.

The Sooty Tern breeds mainly on islands in the Caribbean, Atlantic, Indian and Pacific Oceans. It has received particular attention in the colony known as 'Wideawake Fair' on Ascension Island. The bird has been called the 'Wideawake Tern' because of its perpetual screaming 'ker-wacky-wack', which may be heard at any time of the day or night. The Sooty Tern on Ascension has a breeding cycle of nine and a half months, but elsewhere it is the normal twelve months. On Ascension the birds spend six to seven months at the colony then disappear to sea for three months. The incubation period is about thirty days and fledging is at about five weeks, but the chicks remain in the area for a further eight weeks.

Common Noddy at nest

Three species of terns are usually referred to as 'marsh terns'. The Black Tern (*Chlidonias niger*) breeds in Europe south of the Baltic and eastwards across central Asia, while it also occurs in the central United States and southern Canada. The White-winged Black Tern (*C. leucopterus*) nests eastwards from Hungary to the shores of the China Sea, though in central Asia its range is discontinuous. There have been many sporadic cases of nesting just beyond the edge of its range and many suspected attempts, particularly in the Mediterranean region and in Africa, where there is a distinct possibility that breeding colonies await discovery. The Whiskered Tern (*C. hybrida*) breeds in a number of areas from southern Spain eastwards to India, Australia and New Zealand, and also in southern Africa.

The breeding habits of the White-winged Black Tern are still far from clear. It arrives late in the season, up to three weeks after the Black Tern in the same area. Although it sometimes nests with other marsh species, it tends to keep apart and form sub-colonies. The nest is a platform of reeds plucked by the birds and built up above the water level. That of the Black Tern is a much smaller affair, usually of decaying vegetation, and it may even be constructed of such floating debris. Whiskered Terns' nests are loosely made heaps of reed stems, and may be either afloat or placed in clumps of vegetation. Very little care is taken in nest-building and the structures fall apart quite easily. Though attempts are made to pluck growing reeds these meet with little success, and the birds make use of pieces broken off during the passage of larger animals.

Besides the marsh terns several other species spend most of their time on inland lakes and rivers, rarely going to the sea. Forster's Tern (*S. forsteri*) breeds mainly on inland lakes in western Canada and the United States and moves south to Central America during the winter. It returns to its northern breeding grounds during the early spring to feed on dead fish and invertebrates released by the melting ice. The Indian River Tern (*S. aurantia*) is found on many lakes from Persia eastwards to Burma and the Malay Peninsula. Virtually found in the same area as the Indian River Tern, and often to be seen with it, is the Black-bellied Tern (*S. melanogastes*).

(Top to bottom) Black Tern, Indian River Tern and Whiskered Tern

One of the greatest of bird wanderers is the Arctic Tern (*S. paradisaea*) which nests in a great circumpolar arc about the Arctic regions. It is found to within eight degrees of the North Pole, though at the same time it extends its breeding range southwards to Great Britain and northern France in the eastern Atlantic, and to Massachusetts on the western side. Although a coastal bird, it is also found far inland on moors and tundra and the gravel beaches of lakes and rivers.

The terns return to their nesting grounds during April and May. If in a mixed ternery – the colony is so called when several species breed together – the Arctic Tern will choose the barest ground, though in the absence of competition for nest sites it will use any suitable spot. The size of a colony may vary from one or two pairs nesting on a small skerry to many hundreds scattered over a larger island or tract of moorland.

From studies on the Farne Islands, Northumberland, it has been shown that no Arctic Terns less than three years of age nest, while those doing so for the first time are generally unsuccessful. Those achieving the greatest breeding success were between five or ten years old, though some birds live for

Breeding range, ringed recoveries and sight records of Arctic Tern

● Breeding distribution
● Ringing recoveries in south of birds ringed in north ↓
● Sight or specimen records
↓ (line does not indicate route taken)

Arctic Tern and chicks

as long as twenty. The incubation period seems to be about three weeks and fledging about four weeks. Where colonies are sited on the coast the birds feed on small fish and crustaceans, but if inland a wide variety of insect life is also taken.

During the autumn the birds begin their trans-equatorial migration which takes them to Antarctic regions. It has been said that some Arctic Terns enjoy more hours of daylight than any other animal, for they live during the summer in the land of the midnight sun and many spend the rest of the year in the unending daylight of an Antarctic summer. The journeys undertaken twice yearly by the Arctic Tern will often be 8,000 miles and may reach 11,000 in some cases, a unique undertaking for such a small bird, or, indeed, for any bird.

The Sandwich Tern (*S. sandvicencis*) is only found along the coasts of the United States and Mexico from North Carolina southwards, on European coasts from southern Sweden southwards and in the Black and Caspian Seas. Its major stronghold seems to have been Holland where it is estimated that in the years up until about 1955 between 30,000 and 40,000 pairs nested. This was considered to represent half the European population of the species. Since that date the Dutch population has slumped dramatically to about 500 pairs. It is considered that pesticide residues, found in eggs and dead birds, have been an important contributory factor in this decline. In Great Britain and Ireland the Sandwich Tern population is about 6,000 pairs, with many of these nesting in partly protected areas such as nature reserves. Fortunately, there is so far no evidence for a massive decline in the species such as has occurred in Holland.

Protective measure used in Little Tern nesting colony, at Gibraltar Point, Lincs, England

Sandwich Tern

The Little Tern (*S. albifrons*) is widespread throughout the world, being found in all continents except for South America, and is as much at home on lakes and rivers hundreds of miles inland as it is on the coast. A survey carried out by the Seabird Group in 1967 showed that the total population was then about 1,600 pairs. It is, however, in some difficulties in Great Britain and Ireland where there has been a marked decline in its breeding during the past thirty years. This is most likely due to the fact that virtually all colonies are on the open beach, quite often close to the high-tide mark. In such situations nesting success must be low owing to human disturbance in various forms. If the Little Tern is to survive as a breeding species within the British Isles special protection must be given, and this has now commenced in some areas.

Skimmers

Allied to the terns and gulls is a small, highly interesting group of three species, the skimmers or scissor bills. The Black Skimmer (*Rynchops nigra*), the largest, is some 50 cm (20 in) in length. It is found nesting along the coasts of the United States from New Jersey to Texas and on many coasts in South America southwards to the Argentine. The African Skimmer (*R. flavirostris*), about 43 cm (17 in) in length, is found both on the coasts and inland water systems of Africa, from the Red Sea south to the Orange River. It is no longer found in the Nile Valley. The Indian Skimmer (*R. albicollis*), of similar size to the last species, is found on the rivers and large lakes of Burma and India.

The eye of the skimmer is unique among birds, its pupil being a vertical slit like that of a cat, but the most remarkable feature of these species is the large and characteristic bill. When the chick hatches both mandibles are the same length and can be used to pick up food in the normal manner. However, as the young begin to approach the flying stage the typical adult bill develops. In this the upper mandible is distinctly shorter than the lower, which is very flexible.

The birds rarely alight on the surface of the water but catch their prey, small fish and surface-dwelling aquatic inverte-

Detail of skimmer's bill (left) and in flight 'skimming'

brates, as they fly along very low with the bill open and the lower mandible scooping through the water for several yards. Feeding is normally undertaken at dawn or dusk and during the night when the moon is full. For efficient feeding calm water is essential, and birds may completely desert a river during times of spate.

Skimmers are colonial, though most colonies are small. A typical site is a sand bank where a slight hollow is scooped out for use as a nest. Up to four eggs may be laid; both parents take part in the incubation. The chicks, which can swim well, leave the nest after hatching.

(Top to bottom) Black Skimmer, African Skimmer and Indian Skimmer

Auks in the North Atlantic and North Pacific

- Razorbill
- Common Guillemot
- Brünnich's Guillemot
- Little Auk or Dovekie
- Black Guillemot
- Spectacled Guillemot
- Pigeon Guillemot
- Marbled Murrelet
- Kittlitz's Murrelet

- Cassin's Auklet
- Parakeet Auklet
- Crested Auklet
- Least Auklet
- Whiskered Auklet

- Japanese or Crested Murrelet
- Xantu's Murrelet
- Craveri's Murrelet
- Ancient Murrelet

- Rhinoceros Auklet
- Common Puffin
- Horned Puffin
- Tufted Puffin

Auks

The family of auks or Alcidae are restricted to the colder regions of the northern hemisphere with no representatives in the south. Here their place is taken by the penguins (see pages 18 to 29) and diving petrels (see pages 60 to 63). The majority of species occur in the North Pacific and Bering Sea and sixteen are restricted entirely to these areas. Only six species are found in the North Atlantic, of which three are endemic.

The auks may be divided into seven groups or tribes. The tribe Alcini contains the Razorbill or Razor-billed Auk (*Alca torda*) and the two murres or guillemots, the Common Guillemot (*Uria aalge*) and Brünnich's Guillemot (*Uria lomvia*). The latter species are found in both oceans, the Razorbill only in the North Atlantic.

A single species, the Little Auk or Dovekie (*Plautus alle*), belongs to the tribe Plautini. This bird is about 20 cm (8 in) in length and breeds in Arctic Canada, Greenland, Iceland, Novaya Zemblya, Spitzbergen and Franz Josef Land. Some colonies of this most abundant bird, perhaps the most numerous bird in the North Atlantic, are small, but others are immense. The colony near Thule, Greenland, contains well over a million pairs. With myriads of birds flying and gliding past a cliff, it is very difficult to obtain good estimates of the number present.

The Black Guillemot (*Cepphus grylle*), Pigeon Guillemot (*C. columba*), sometimes considered only as a race of the former species, and the Spectacled Guillemot (*C. carbo*) are members of the tribe Cepphini.

The three species of puffin, two occurring in the North Pacific, the third in the North Atlantic, belong to the tribe Fraterculini. Closely related to these are the auklets of the North Pacific, the five species of the tribe Aethini.

The last two tribes are both comprised of murrelets, again species which are found only in the North Pacific and Bering Sea area. The tribe Brachyramphini has two species, the Marbled Murrelet (*B. marmoratus*) and Kittlitz's Murrelet (*B. brevirostris*). The tribe Synthliboramphini contains the remaining four species.

Distribution of the auk family

The Great Auk (*Pinguinis impennis*) or the Garefowl, as it is sometimes known, is, or rather was, the largest of its family, for unfortunately it has now been extinct for over a century. Standing some 76 cm (30 in) high the Great Auk resembled a giant Razorbill except that it was flightless, a fact which helped to spell its doom. It was the original 'penguin', a name which was handed on later to that well-known group of birds from the southern hemisphere.

From the remains of the Great Auk found in numerous cave deposits and kitchen middens throughout north-west Europe and the Mediterranean region, it is evident that this bird was formerly a source of food.

Only eight breeding places of the Great Auk are definitely known while about a dozen further sites are suspected. Undoubtedly the birds also nested elsewhere. The main population centre seems to have been in the Newfoundland area, judging by the reports of explorers like Jaques Cartier who arrived in the region during 1534. Later accounts tell of birds being taken by the boatload for food by ships' crews, the hapless auks being driven up planks or across sails straight on board the vessels. The slaughter was so immense that by about 1800 the Great Auk was extinct as a breeding bird in Newfoundland.

In Europe the Great Auk nested on St Kilda until the latter half of the seventeenth century and a tutor to the laird of the island has left a description of the bird and its habits. It was on one of the great sea stacks of St Kilda, Stac an Armin, that in 1840 the last Great Auk to be seen alive in British waters was clubbed to death by two islanders who thought they had en-

Breeding areas of the Great Auk

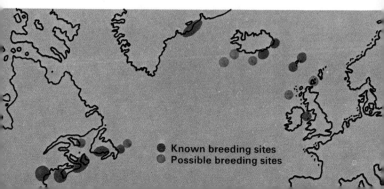

Known breeding sites
Possible breeding sites

countered a witch. It would seem, therefore, that at that date the unfortunate bird was already a most unusual occurrence in those waters.

The doom of the Great Auk was finally sealed on June 4th, 1844, on the island of Eldey, Iceland, when two Great Auks were killed and the single egg smashed. Since that day none has been seen alive, though many searched during the mid-nineteenth century without success. Man's ignorance and greed were responsible for the extermination of a most remarkable species of seabird.

Great Auk

Razorbill with chick

Most members of the family Alcidae are colonial species and some are found in immense colonies. A colony of Brünnich's Guillemot at Cape Shackleton, West Greenland, probably contains a million pairs, half the Greenland population of this bird. The Black Guillemot on the other hand, though it is found in small colonies, may often nest in solitary pairs with a considerable distance between each.

Nest sites vary, the Common and Brünnich's Guillemots using ledges, which are often exceedingly narrow, while the Razorbill tends to use crevices and hollows beneath boulders. Others, notably the puffins, are burrow-nesters. One or two eggs are laid, depending on the species, and both parents take part in the incubation. Chicks are covered in down on hatching

Xantu's Murrelet and chick (left) and Atlantic Puffin with young

and those of one of the murrelet tribes are truly remarkable in that they leave the nest when only a few days old to go to sea. Even at that early stage, they have enormous feet almost the size of their parents.

The chicks of other species, like the Razorbill, stay on the nest ledge or crevice until they are between two and three weeks old and a third of the size of their parents before leaving. This they usually do at dusk, urged down to the sea, perhaps hundreds of feet below, by the agitated cries of their parents swimming about on the water.

The chicks of the puffins, safe below ground in a burrow, take things much more leisurely and do not leave its safety until they are fully grown and feathered.

Horned Puffin (left)
and Tufted Puffin

The Atlantic Puffin (*Fratercula arctica*) occurs in the North Atlantic, while the remaining two species, the Tufted Puffin (*Lunda cirrhota*) and the Horned Puffin (*F. corniculata*), are found in the North Pacific.

Puffins are the most comical of birds, always curious as to what their neighbours are doing. This often leads to duels when their huge beaks are used to grip on opponent's leg or wing. These encounters may be very prolonged and if near to a cliff edge both birds may fall over, only to break apart before reaching the rocks or sea below.

Not only does the Horned Puffin quarrel with others, it also seems to carry on a protracted argument with its mate. Such arguments are often carried on in the nest chamber from which angry growling and scolding noises may be heard.

Atlantic Puffin
and map showing
breeding areas

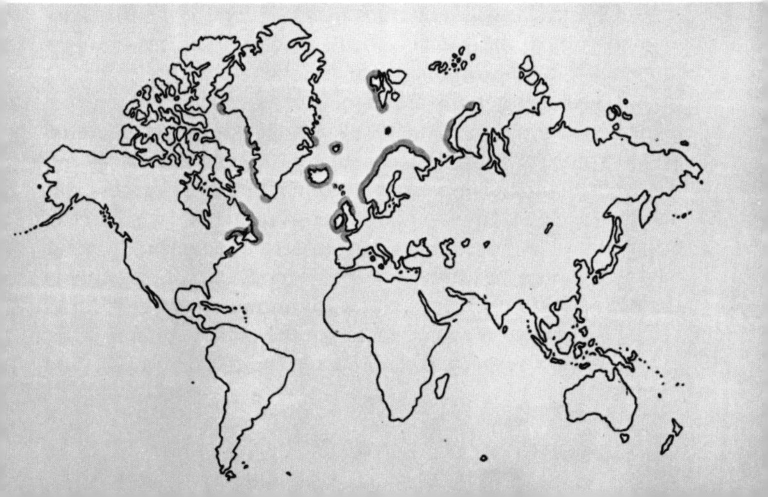

The Common Guillemot is a species which, at least in the eastern Atlantic, seems to be decreasing at many colonies, particularly those in the southern section of its range. Changes in temperature, which in turn affect the food supply, and pollution of the sea seem to be major contributory factors in this decline.

Although their breeding season is relatively short – approximately May to July – Guillemots visit the cliffs over a much wider period. Probably the only months when they do not land are August (except for delayed breeders), September and October. During the winter months, in suitable calm weather, large numbers of the birds will visit the colony in the hours soon after dawn, often for only a brief time. These irregular visits which continue with increasing regularity until the onset of breeding are still the subject of speculation among ornithologists.

The Common Guillemot occurs in two forms, the normal and the 'ringed' or 'bridled' form. The bridled Guillemot was at one time considered erroneously to have been a separate species. Since the 1930s several surveys into the occurrence of the bridled Guillemot have been conducted by H. N. Southern. They have established that the bridled form is absent from the Pacific Ocean, being found only in Atlantic colonies. Here the enquiries revealed that the percentage of bridled birds is one per cent or less in the south of England and on the coasts of France. As colonies to the north are examined it soon becomes apparent that the percentage increases, so that in south-west Ireland over fifty per cent of the birds are bridled. With the survey being carried out at ten-year intervals it has been possible to see changes taking place. At first it seemed that the frequency of occurrence of bridled birds was declining, an amelioration of climate being suggested as a reason. However, a later survey showed that the trend had been completely reversed although the climatic conditions had not changed. Now, with further information to hand from other countries, it seems as if the areas occupied by birds having the same percentage of bridled individuals may follow the distribution of surface-water isotherms.

The three species which make up the tribe Cepphini differ in a number of respects from others in the auk family. On land

Common Guillemot (top), Brünnich's Guillemot (bottom left) and Bridled Guillemot

they do not stand nearly so upright, and when at rest their posture is almost duck-like. They have only weak, though often high-pitched, calls.

The nest sites are usually among boulders and in crevices, often in dark cave recesses, while in several localities holes in harbour walls have been used. Because of their more solitary nature and because they tend to nest thinly spread along a

Spectacled Guillemot (left) and Pigeon Guillemot

coast, not nearly so much is known about their numbers and distribution. In Great Britain and Ireland the Black Guillemot is found in both the Orkneys and Shetlands, down the west coast of Scotland, in the north Irish Sea area and in many places round Ireland. Birds have been reported during recent summers in south-west Wales and this together with other records seems to indicate an expansion in western Britain.

The Cepphini lay two eggs, having two brood-spots in comparison with several species of auk which lay one egg and have a single brood-spot. The incubation period seems to be between twenty-seven and thirty days. The chicks remain at the

Little Auk (left) and Black Guillemot

nest site until they are about five weeks old and fully grown. During the winter the Cepphini change into a greyish-white ghost-like plumage.

The Little Auk, in a tribe all on its own nests in the Arctic regions in large colonies. These are usually found near the base of steep slopes, though the birds may go up beyond the snow-line to a height of 500 m (1,500 ft). Other colonies may be on inland cliffs as much as twenty miles from the sea.

The birds move south during the winter, with huge numbers congregating on the Grand Banks, Newfoundland. Smaller numbers are found off west European coasts.

The murrelets, of which there are six species belong to two tribes. All are small birds between 20 cm (8 in) and 25 cm (10 in) in length.

The Marbled Murrelet is still a bird of mystery in that only a single egg is known to science, and that was taken from the oviduct of a shot female. The nest site has never been found, though the bird is numerous on the coasts of Alaska and British Columbia and in the islands eastwards to Kamchatka. From the evidence it seems that the birds fly inland, perhaps many miles, to nest in the high timber lands, but the virtual inaccessibility of the terrain makes the possible discovery of a colony tremendously difficult.

Kittlitz's Murrelet is another species that flies far inland to nest and seems to do so on bare ground, among rocks and snow, above the timberline in Alaska, and the islands across the North Pacific. A nest site of this species was not discovered until 1913.

The Japanese or Crested Murrelet (*Synthliboramphus wumizusume*) nests on the coasts of Japan. Xantu's Murrelet (*Endo-*

Ancient Murrelet (left) and Marbled Murrelet in summer plumage

mychura hypoleucus) nests on islands off California. It lays one or two eggs in mid-March, using crevices among boulders or even the cover of dense bushes as nest sites. No material is used at the nest. Birds use suitable spots from just above the high-water mark to way up mountain sides. The young are led to sea by their parents within a few days of hatching, and even at this early stage can swim and dive with amazing skill.

Craveri's Murrelet (*E. craveri*) is considered by some authorities to be only the southern race of the previous species. It nests on islands in the Gulf of California, where the breeding season commences in February, and like Xantu's Murrelet it is nocturnal at the breeding colonies.

The Ancient Murrelet (*S. antiquus*) resides much further north in Alaska and across the Bering Sea. The nest is usually in a burrow, two eggs being laid. Nocturnal at its breeding grounds, the Ancient Murrelet has a call like that of a Leach's Petrel except that it is higher pitched.

Kittlitz's Murrelet in summer plumage

Cassin's Auklet
(left), Rhinoceros
Auklet (centre)
and Crested
Auklet

The six auklets are also small species. The Least Auklet (*Aethia pusilla*) is barely 17 cm (7 in) in length, while the Rhinoceros Auklet (*Cerorhinca monocerata*) is the largest at some 35 cm (14 in) long. This bird gets its name from the blunt horn at the base of the beak. During April the birds return to their colonies along the western coasts of Canada and the United States as far south as Washington and on islands west to Kamchatka. They are nocturnal birds when ashore and are noisy when they first arrive. Later, as the breeding season commences, the colonies are silent except for the whirring of short wings. The nest, lined with dead grass, is at the end of a tunnel which may be up to 6 m (20 ft) in length though it is usually between 1·50 m (5 ft) and 2·50 m (8 ft). In this a single egg is laid late in May.

The Crested Auklet (*A. cristatella*) breeds on the Pribilof, Aleutian and Shumagin Islands and in south-west Alaska. Because of its flight, size and colour it has received the local name 'sea-quail'. During May these auklets return to their breeding

Least Auklet (left), Parakeet Auklet (centre) and Whiskered Auklet

colonies which are usually to be found on prominent headlands where there is a conglomeration of boulders just above high-water mark. Both parents take turns in the incubation of the single egg, the precise period of which is not known. The young remain hidden away until they can fly.

The Whiskered Auklet (*A. pygmaea*) is probably the rarest and least known of the tribe. It nests in the Aleutian Islands and is seldom seen any great distance from the colonies. The Parakeet Auklet (*Cyclorrhynchus psittacula*) breeds from northeast Siberia through the Bering Sea islands to Alaska. It is a very tame or, perhaps, fearless species which nests in burrows among rocks.

Cassin's Auklet (*Ptychoramphus aleuticus*), a nocturnal species, has the widest breeding range of all, being found south from the Aleutian Islands to central California. It is very numerous on some islands, and nests not only in natural crevices but under driftwood and even among sacks of coal. It seems to have a prolonged breeding season.

OTHER MARITIME SPECIES

In the preceding pages the groups of birds generally accepted as seabirds have been briefly discussed. However, it is obvious that a number of species from different groups are far from being maritime in their habits. Some of the gulls and terns in particular are restricted to inland lakes and river systems.

There are, however, other seabirds which lay strong claim to being thought of as seabirds, particularly the three species of phalarope. Wilson's Phalarope (*Steganopus tricolor*), the largest at about 25 cm (10 in) in length, is the least pelagic of the three. The names of the other two species are different, depending on which side of the Atlantic one is, and can lead to confusion. The Grey Phalarope (*Phalaropus fulicarius*), named after its grey winter plumage, is the Red Phalarope in America after its summer dress. The Red-necked Phalarope (*Lobipes lobatus*) of Europe becomes the Northern Phalarope in America. In this account the appropriate European names will be used.

Both species are circumpolar in their distribution with some overlapping in range. However, the Red-necked extends further south in summer than does the Grey. All three species have an unusual spinning action during feeding. They turn quickly round on the surface of the water, picking up floating organisms and small invertebrates which are carried to the top by the turbulence created.

Both the Red-necked and the Grey Phalaropes spend the winter at sea, moving southwards in both the Pacific and Atlantic Oceans to areas of a rich plankton supply. The Red-necked is a more tropical species in winter, while the Grey Phalarope continues south to temperate zones. Well-favoured winter areas for both species include an area off West Africa north of the Equator, off Angola and south-west Africa, Peru, Arabian waters and the south-west Pacific.

It is not surprising that such small birds, wandering the world's oceans, should occasionally suffer disasters when large numbers are carried on to coasts and inland by severe weather. In Newfoundland they are known by the local name 'gale-birds'.

Red-necked Phalarope

The duck family has among its many members several that are more or less maritime in their habits. In northern Europe one of the most frequent birds to be seen along rocky coasts is the Eider Duck (*Somateria mollissima*). It has a discontinuous circumpolar distribution going beyond eighty degrees north in several places. In Europe there has been an expansion of range southwards in recent years. The birds often congregate in large colonies, and one in Greenland contains some 10,000 pairs. The down, which in Iceland is harvested from nests, is of the purest quality.

The three species of scoter are also largely marine, only coming ashore to nest. The Velvet Scoter (*Melanitta fusca*) has a circumpolar distribution though rarely goes beyond the tree-line. They breed on inland lakes, often in mountainous areas, but move to the sea during winter months. The Common Scoter (*M. nigra*) is found right across northern Europe and Asia and in Alaska. Following the breeding season it spends its time continually at sea, normally in coastal areas where it feeds on bivalves taken from the sea-bed.

The four species of diver or loon belong to the family Gaviidae. Two, the Red-throated Diver (*Gavia stellata*) and the Black-throated Diver (*G. arctica*) are circumpolar in their distribution. The former is the more widespread species, though both extend from the Arctic regions south to Scotland and, in the case of the former, to western Ireland. During the winter months both move south, and in favourite bays large flocks may sometimes gather.

The other species, the Great Northern Diver (*G. immer*) and the White-billed Diver (*G. adamsii*) are not quite so widespread. The former is found over a large area of the northern United States and Canada, part of Greenland and Iceland. The latter occurs in northern Finland, east along the coasts of Russia and Siberia, Alaska and northern Canada. It does not seem to move very far south in winter and there are very few records of its occurring in Britain or other temperate European countries.

Eider Duck (left) and Black-throated Diver

Several members of the waders, or shorebirds as they are termed in North America, have some claim to be thought of as seabirds. The majority only frequent the coast during the off-season months, though some may breed on beaches, among sand dunes and in coastal marshes.

Two of the most unusual species are the sheathbills of the family Chionididae. These are the only birds with unwebbed feet which reach the shores of the Antarctic continent. They are found in large numbers on many islands in Antarctic waters, ranging from Tierra del Fuego and the Falklands eastwards to those in the Indian Ocean sector. Rather pigeon-like in appearance, they have all-white plumage and pink eyes, with a peculiar yellow wattling on the cheeks, and thick-set, short, grey legs. The wings are short and have sharp spurs on the carpal joint, used when the birds fight.

Although they are seen from time to time many hundreds of miles from land, most seem to spend their time along the shore-line, often scavenging about expedition bases, while in the past every whaling station must have supported a large population of these birds. They feed on any debris, decaying animal or vegetable matter that can be found. If this is not available they will take any of the small marine animals along the shore-line. Round penguin colonies they are a particular menace. They take eggs and small chicks and will pick up scraps of food left after the chicks are fed. One habit which they have developed is for one of a pair to distract an adult penguin from feeding its chick by pecking at it, causing the penguin to drop the food which the other sheathbill promptly snatches.

Although flocking together in large numbers, sheathbills tend to be more solitary when nesting. The normal site seems to be among boulders often close to a penguin colony. Two, sometimes three eggs, are laid. These take about twenty-eight days to hatch, with both parents assisting in the incubation.

The chicks, covered in grey down at first, assume adult plumage before leaving the nest. During the winter months the southernmost population of these unusual birds moves northwards, while those on the islands seem much more sedentary.

Sheathbill

BOOKS TO READ

The following books are recommended for further reading. Although some are now out of print, they have not been superceded by more recent publications and are probably available from public libraries.

The only identification book which contains information about all the seabirds of the world is:
Birds of the Ocean by W. B. Alexander. Putnam, London, 1928.

Many of the regional field guides are excellent for their own areas, for instance:
A Field Guide to the Birds of Great Britain and Europe by Roger Peterson, Guy Mountfort and P. A. D. Hollom. Collins, London, 1954.
A Guide to Field Identification: Birds of North America by Chandler S. Robbins, Bertel Bruun and Herbert S. Zim. Golden Press, New York, 1966.
Birds of the Atlantic Ocean by Ted Stokes. Country Life, London, 1968.

Of a more general nature *Seabirds* by James Fisher and R. M. Lockley, published by Collins, London, 1954, in the New Naturalist Series is excellent, while for the younger reader, although it should not be neglected by adults, *Seabirds* by M. E. Gilham in the Instructions to Young Ornithologists Series published by the Museum Press, London, 1963 is of value.

Turning now to more specific details, a number of monographs on seabird species or groups are available and are a 'must' for the marine naturalist:
The Fulmar by James Fisher. New Naturalist, No. 6, Collins, London, 1952.
The Herring Gull's World by Niko Tinbergen. New Naturalist, No. 9, Collins, London, 1953.
The Murres, their Distribution, Populations and Biology by Leslie M. Tuck. Canadian Fish and Wildlife Service, Ottowa, 1960.
Penguins by John Sparks and Tony Soper. David and Charles, Newton Abbot, 1964.
Shearwaters by R. M. Lockley. Dent, London, 1947.

INDEX

Figures in bold type refer to illustrations.

SOME OTHER TITLES IN THIS SERIES

Natural History

The Animal Kingdom
Animals of Australia & New Zealand
Animals of Southern Asia
Bird Behaviour
Birds of Prey

Evolution of Life
Fishes of the World
Fossil Man
A Guide to the Seashore

Gardening

Chrysanthemums

Garden Flowers

Popular Science

Astronomy
Atomic Energy
Computers at Work

The Earth
Electricity
Electronics

Arts

Architecture

Jewellery

General Information

Arms and Armour
Coins
Flags

Guns
Military Uniforms
Rockets and Missiles

Domestic Animals & Pets

Budgerigars
Cats

Dog Care
Dogs

Domestic Science

Flower Arranging

History & Mythology

Archaeology
Discovery of
   Africa
   Australia
   Japan

Discovery of
   North America
   South America
   The American West